I know only a handful of pastors who move with a deep-seated passion to communicate the rich treasures of God's Word to a hurting world, like my friend, Ken Johnson. I'm thrilled that his profound message and spiritual insight will soon become life on the printed page. What Ken has to say should be printed everywhere, from the *Wall Street Journal* and *USA Today* to the bulletin board at the corner market.

—Dr. Ron Mehl
Beloved late senior pastor of
Beaverton Foursquare Church
author of *God Works the Night Shift*

The "Son-light" Ken Johnson's work radiates comes with a warmth and power that can burn away the fog of uncertainty and confusion that so often clouds our sense of personal purpose. *Life²* is going to clear and focus an "on-target" life for a lot of people.

—Jack W. Hayford
President, Foursquare International

This easy read by Ken Johnson compels you to see our lives as God sees them—immense, glorious, and alive in Christ! It's time we right-size Jesus and downsize our doubts. The results will be nothing short of a revelation!

—Wayne Cordeiro

In *Life²* Ken shares more than merely philosophy and theory to take your life to the next level. He shows you how to do it…step by step! This inspiring book will be your blueprint to transforming your relationships, your faith, and even your business. His experience as a business leader before he became a pastor provides "real world" traction to this God-inspired eternal message of success in life.

—Dirk Zeller, CEO of Sales Champions
Author of *Telephone Sales for Dummies*,
The Champion Agent, and *The Champion Team*

I rarely read something that I just can't put down. *Life²* had me turning pages! Ken Johnson's zeal for the abundant life is not only clear, it's contagious.

—Kelly Talamo
Consultant, Speaker, and President
Men Step Up Ministries
Atlanta, GA

Life²

Life²

Ken Johnson

Foursquare Media

Life² by Ken Johnson
Published by Foursquare Media
1910 W. Sunset Blvd., Suite 200
Los Angeles, California 90026

This book is produced and distributed by Creation House, a part of Strang Communications, www.creationhouse.com.

Copyright © 2007 by Ken Johnson
All rights reserved

Library of Congress Control Number: 2007940829
International Standard Book Number: 978-1-59979-294-1

First Edition

07 08 09 10 11 — 987654321
Printed in the United States of America

This book is dedicated to my father, Bob Johnson, who is a man's man and a man of God. Thanks Dad, for believing in me and in God's plan for my life, even when I was so far from God and so far from what you taught me that only faith could see a blessed future for me. Thanks for being faithful to Mom, to Jesus Christ, and to your family for all these years.

ACKNOWLEDGMENTS

I'm reminded of the six-year-old boy who woke up because he heard a thump in the dark and cried out for his dad. His dad ran to his room, sat on his bed, reassured him, prayed with him, and got up to leave. "Daddy, don't go," the boy said, "I'm scared." "You don't need to be afraid," his dad said, "Jesus is here." After a few moments of dark silence, the boy replied, "Yes, but I need Jesus with skin."

I am so blessed to have Jesus-with-skin-people in my life. One of them is my friend Larry Libby, a gifted word-crafter, who helped me and encouraged me as I wrote this book. Next, I thank my patient wife, Linda, who deserves official sainthood for loving me these thirty-six years, warts and all. I must also thank Westside Church, all of you, for staying awake while I preach and for seeing through me to Christ. I love doing life with you. I want to thank Rick Wulfestieg, head of Foursquare Media, who looks and sounds a lot like Jesus. Finally, I heartily thank Pastor Jack Hayford for leading our global family of churches, like David of old, with "a true heart and skillful hands" (Psalm 78:72).

CONTENTS

Foreword xv

1 A Modest Proposal 1

2 A Walk Under the Stars 7

3 Overcoming Gravity 27

4 Death Grip 43

5 Life With a View 65

6 Fountain of Youth 85

7 Dead Men Walking 97

8 A Better Country 117

FOREWORD

God created you and has a wonderful plan for your life. Undoubtedly you are familiar with the concept; are you living in that reality?

My friend Ken Johnson crafted the book you are about to read to entice you, challenge you, even persuade you, to live the full, rich life God has in mind for you.

I have known Ken and his wife, Linda, for over twenty-five years. When I first met Ken he had long hair, a beard, and a radically optimistic view of the potential of the church and of the possibilities of a person who lives life with a passion—pursuing obedience to Jesus Christ. He was a bit "on the edge," and I loved that about him. In the ensuing years, Ken has not lost his passion for Jesus or the church. I have watched, up close and personal, how Ken has lived his life as a pastor, leader, husband, father, and friend. Believe me, this is a man who lives life to the fullest.

I am confident that the insights Ken offers from Scripture, as well as his personal experience, will motivate you to move toward the life God has purposed for you, the full, abundant life Jesus promised. This is not a life of ease, but a life that takes on the challenges we all face, full of faith, full of God's Spirit, and directed by the principles and eternal truths of God's Word.

Hang on; you are in for an adventure!

—STAN SIMMONS

CHAPTER 1

A MODEST PROPOSAL

Messages beyond number, shrill and calm, foolish and wise, audible and inaudible, visible and invisible, comprehensible and incomprehensible, surround you and envelop you at this precise moment.

You are swimming, but not in water.

You are swimming in messages.

Sure, there are all the expected ones: conversations, phone calls, newspaper stories, Internet blogs, e-mails, billboards, and so forth. Maybe you'll pick up a magazine or a book and collect a few more. All the usual outlets.

That's obvious enough. But it's only the beginning.

At this instant—shooting above you, dancing around you, and flowing right *through* you—electronic messages fill the air like a cloud of Minnesota mosquitoes. And in the spiritual realm—perhaps occupying the same "space" as our physical world, countless additional communications move along their mysterious trajectories. The songs of angels and the mutterings of demons. The sweet voice of God's Holy Spirit.

Among all of those trillions of messages, this little book adds one more. One rather modest proposal to place in front of you. Worth your while? I think so. But you be the judge.

Here's the quick version.

God, who invented life, loves life, and *is* life, offers you more life than what you currently possess.

In other words, in addition to the life you already have, the Bible says there is more. Longer life? Perhaps, but not just that. More life. Better life.

That's about it, and it either interests you or it doesn't.

That's one message among the multiplied hosts you will encounter today. But there it is.

Jesus Christ claimed that His mission on this planet was to bring me, bring you, the possibility of *more life*. In one translation of John 10:10, we read:

> I came so they can have real and eternal life, more and better
> life than they ever dreamed of.
> —JOHN 10:10, THE MESSAGE

Do you believe the Bible? Do you believe that the lungs of a man named Jesus actually pushed out spent air one day, caused His vocal chords to vibrate, and that He shaped His mouth and tongue to form the words, *"More and better life than they ever dreamed of"*?

Well, you say, you quoted that verse in a paraphrase of scripture. No problem. Look it up in the translation of your choice.

> I have come that they may have life, and have it to the full
> (NIV).

> I have come that they may have life, and that they may have
> it more abundantly (NKJV).

> My purpose is to give life in all its fullness (TLB).

I came to bring life, and far more life than before (Phillips).

I came that they may have and enjoy life, and have it in abundance (to the full, till it overflows) (AMP).

Крадецът влиза само да открадне, да заколи и да погуби; Аз дойдох за да имат живот, и да го имат изобилно (The New Testament in Bulgarian).[1]

It all adds up to the same thing doesn't it? Whatever the precise phrasing, do you believe He actually said it? I do. I believe it with all of my heart. I believe He stated His mission just that way because our Creator wired us to want a better life. It's the common human DNA.

I also believe that most Christ-followers are settling for less than the tip of the iceberg on this "better life" promise. We go to great ends to experience better, richer, fuller, longer, larger life. We live for those moments where our soul cries out, "This is living!" For some of us, those moments don't come very often. Not nearly often enough.

As important as these thought things might be, they can be challenging to grab hold of sometimes. Like a bar of slippery soap in the shower.

That's why the concepts have to be anchored on familiar ground. And the ground I have chosen is the life of Abraham, "the father of our faith." (See Romans 4.) It's a story of blood and sweat, tears and joys, sorrows and wisdom, colossal mistakes and giant steps of faith. It's messy because life is messy—and this is life as real as it gets.

It begins with Abraham hearing a little voice that you've heard, too. Something from somewhere high above him or deep inside him that whispered, "There's more."

I believe God put such a voice in every human being. That voice (unless gagged, stuffed in a back closet, or drowned out by ceaseless noise) whispers over and over, day after day, deep in your soul. The voice pleads with us, begging us not to accept a life of bland, bloodless, colorless resignation. Can you hear it? There's more...more to this thing called life...more than you've even begun to realize.

Thousands of years ago God offered a man named Abraham a superior life, a second life:

> I will make you into a great nation and I will bless you; I will make your name great, and you will be a blessing. I will bless those who bless you.
>
> —Genesis 12:2–3

This was no try-a-new-career or take-a-class-at-community-college. This was a radical departure from all this man had ever known.

It was quite a proposition, wasn't it? You'll be blessed. Those whom bless you will be blessed. You yourself will be a blessing. Blessings, blessings, and more blessings. Better life galore.

Maybe you've heard about a tribe of nomads called Tartars. They were herders who were always in search of new pasture. As a result, they kept moving and moving. As soon as the grass was grazed in one area, they moved to another region. The very worst swear word they had, their worst curse, was simply this: "May you stay in one place the rest of your life."

That was their equivalent of "Go to hell."

Never moving, never finding fresh pasture, never seeing over the horizon—staying in one place forever. Now that I think about it, it does sound hellish.

When I was a little kid, some distant relatives from Missouri would come out to the Pacific Northwest and visit my family in Oregon every few summers. They would gawk at the trees, travel to the mountains, gush about the green, stand on a cliff overlooking the Pacific, and say, "You know, we've just got to leave 'Misery' one of these days." That's what they jokingly called their home state.

I'm sure Missouri is a fine place. I've never been there. But I do know that some people live in a state of perpetual misery simple because they aren't willing to pay the price of uncertainty and leave their familiar confines.

> The Lord had said to Abram, "Leave your country, your people and your father's household and go to the land I will show you."
>
> —GENESIS 12:1

It was a test. Would Abraham respond to the call, leaving behind all he knew and most of what he had to follow God into the unknown?

Leave your country. Leave your people. Leave your relatives. Leave your house. That's a whole lot of leavin'. God didn't even give Abraham an AAA map. He didn't show him a postcard or travel brochure. His destination was up in the air. It was the "go now, know later" plan. He was asked to leave everything that he had spent his life growing accustomed to, everything familiar.

The word *familiar* has the same root as the word *family*. Like family members, familiar things are well-known. We're accustomed to them. At home with them. They fit. They feel right. Comfortable.

The problem is, we can get so accustomed to the familiar that we get stuck in our comfort zone. We can get cozy with life as we know it and refuse to venture out into the land of adventure.

> By faith Abraham, when called to go...obeyed and went, even though he did not know where he was going.
> —HEBREWS 11:8

Abraham could have lived under house arrest the rest of his life, but he didn't. He walked off the edge of his known world.

To follow God off your map like Abraham did, you have to rebuke a "settler" mentality and always be a pioneer. Don't settle for things as they are, aspire for things as God meant them to be. Believe Jesus Christ when He says, "There's more!"

Are insecurity, fear, convention, and small thinking causing you to settle for what you have? Are you claiming sanctuary in the familiar, or are you willing to follow God around a blind corner? Abraham's adventure began when he left Famili-Ur. And yours will, too.

> God told him [Abram], "Leave your own country behind you, and your own people, and go to the land I will guide you to. If you do...."
> —GENESIS 12:1–2, TLB

That's the biggest "if" in life. And it may start with turning the next page.

What follows are five key moments in the life of Abraham, and what he learned about something I call *Life²*.

CHAPTER 2

A WALK UNDER
THE STARS

Times of fear, change, and transition may offer doorways
to life at a higher level.

My friend Rick started a hobby of hang gliding back
in 1976. At the time the sport consisted of more or
less running off the top of a hill and gliding to the
bottom.

Thirty years ago that was about as daring as it got. If you could
have told one of those pioneer gliders how the sport would evolve
in the next thirty years, I wonder if they would even believe you.

The technology and equipment has so changed and improved
that enthusiasts have gone far beyond mere gliding from hilltops.
That's sissy stuff. Now it's a soaring sport, and people fly for miles
across country, riding currents of wind like high-flying eagles. Rick
has flown as high as 18,000 feet on a launch from the Sierras—a
far cry from jumping off the 600-foot butte south of town—and
has traveled as far as 197 miles in one flight.

Back in 2003, Rick was soaring somewhere over the south-
eastern Oregon desert when he looked down and saw a dust devil

far below him. Dust devils, he later explained to me, indicate the presence of a thermal, and may top out as high as 1,000 to 2,000 feet.

Rick was soaring at about 10,500 feet when he spotted the phenomenon. Immediately he was interested. On that particular day he wanted to get up into the cloud base, at about 13,500 feet. To do that, he needed a lift. So he decided to see it he could get a little boost from a handy thermal associated with the dust devil churning through the desert far below.

He got the lift all right. But he also ran into a patch of turbulence so severe that it shook his teeth. Most likely you've been on board a 737 when the pilot announces "a little turbulence up ahead." He will usually say something bland and non-threatening like, "Well, folks, I'm turning the seat belt sign back on for a bit, because it could get a little bumpy up ahead."

Bumpy? When you are the fuselage of the plane and the wings are strapped to your arms, "bumpy" just doesn't describe it. Turbulence at 10,500 feet in a hang glider puts an entirely different slant on the issue. Rick was being shaken hard. Like a rag doll. Hoping to find smoother, faster rising air in the center of the thermal, he angled for the middle.

That's when the bottom dropped out of everything.

Hitting the mother of all air pockets, Rick suddenly felt weightless. At the same moment, he heard a loud popping sound. And then he felt himself plunging to the earth like a guided missile, one wing folded down and useless.

Perilously close to blacking out, he finally managed to jerk the ripcord on his parachute—and the shock of the opening red canopy almost knocked the wind out of him. Yes, the chute was open, but he had fallen like a cannon ball through the summer sky, and it could have very well been too late to save himself.

In a minute and a half, he plunged nearly 11,000 feet and into the branches of a tree, his feet dangling less than a foot off the ground.

In fact, it happened to be the only tree in sight. But it had caught him and kept him from hitting the desert floor with much too great a velocity; it saved his life.

Later on when he had time to think about those harrowing moments, Rick said two things came to mind. First, that life is tenuous. One minute you're riding high, gliding along through the clouds, following your flight plan, and the next minute you're plunging toward your death. The second thing Rick realized was that the incident had happened for a purpose.

"Obviously," Rick reflected, "God wants me alive for some reason—and hopefully He'll let me know what that is someday." The Lord had allowed His servant to literally drop from the clouds, and caught him two feet from the ground.

I'm so glad God is with us through any elevation. Even though we may be committed, Spirit-filled followers of Jesus Christ, it's a plain fact of life that we're going to have some lows mixed in with our highs and our mediums. We're bound to experience some mundane times and dry times, frightening times and lonely times.

And God wants to be with us in all of the highs and all of the lows.

Perhaps you find yourself in a bit of a down time as you read these words, and you've been wondering how to get out of that downward spiral. You're not alone in those thoughts. In fact, even Abraham, the father of our faith, experienced those moments in life when a promising thermal dropped him right into a bottom-less air pocket.

Ups and Downs

Abraham left Ur and plunged ahead into the unknown, just as God had commanded. But there was a stopover. He pitched his tents at Haran with a few of his closest relatives. Haran was his halfway house, somewhere between familiar Ur and his ordained destination. Then one day, with some fresh prompting from God, he took the full plunge. He loaded his wife, his nephew Lot, and his furniture in a Mid-East U-Haul and "set out for the land of Canaan" (Gen. 12:5).

What happens when a person gets to where God told them to go? Does he get some kind of heavenly rush or spiritual high and just stay up there with eagles? Abraham sure didn't.

According to my chronological Bible, chapters 12–14 of Genesis cover a period of about fifteen years.[1] Abraham had some real ups and downs in that decade and a half. The Lord appeared to him at Shechem. That was so uplifting he built two altars to the Lord. Then came a famine. That's a downer. From there things went south, and so did Abraham. Down in Egypt he protected his own life at the expense of his wife. His cowardly dishonesty almost took his marriage down.

But there were some ups in Egypt. For one, both Abraham and Lot played the market well and got plenty of stock. Good stock. Livestock. Their net worth was on the ascendancy.

Then they left Egypt and went north to Canaan. They were prosperous now, but prosperity has its challenges. Abraham and Lot had more flocks and herds than their grazing permit could pasture. After a family feud and a few rangeland fights, they agreed to a stock split and went their separate ways.

That's when Abraham did an interesting thing.

Even though he was Lot's uncle, Lot's elder, he let Lot take first pick of pasture. It usually doesn't work that way in the Middle East. Seniors have seniority. But Abraham was beginning to learn how to loosen his grip on his blessings. The man from Ur was starting to catch on to this "life at a whole new level" thing. He was starting to figure out that if he would focus on being generous with others, God would be very generous with him.

Abram was learning, but Lot was not. Lot's choices placed him and his family in the wrong place at the wrong time, drawing them into deep and desperate trouble.

"Trouble in the Mid-East" is nothing new, of course. I believe the same evil spirits that keep the turmoil and hatred alive in that corner of the world today were active all the way back in Abraham's day. And somewhere around 2091 BC, a great battle was brewing in what would one day be the land of Israel.[2] To put it briefly, an alliance of four kings made war against an alliance of five kings—and the four-king-alliance won the day. In the process, the victors looted the twin sin cities on the plain of the Jordan—Sodom and Gomorrah—getting away with the booty and kidnapping some of the people.

Abraham probably couldn't have cared less about a bunch of pagan kings battling it out, and just went about his business. What did Canaanite politics have to do with him? But then came word that his nephew Lot—and probably Lot's wife and girls—had been taken captive by the victorious kings.

Now it was a family matter.

And Abraham wasn't about to let that stick.

> When Abram heard that his nephew had been taken prisoner, he lined up his servants, all of them born in his household—there were 318 of them—and chased after the captors all the way to Dan. Abram and his men split into small groups and attacked by night. They chased them as far as Hobah, just north of Damascus. They recovered all the plunder along with nephew Lot and his possessions, including the women and the people.
>
> —GENESIS 14:14–16, THE MESSAGE

So Abraham and a few hundred men of his household attacked an alliance of four armies, whipped them soundly, and chased them all the way into what would one day become Syria. No problem, right? All in a day's work.

Then, after extracting Lot and his family from captivity, Abraham refused to accept a personal reward from the grateful king of Sodom, moving on to a mysterious encounter with the priest-king of Salem—a man the Scriptures call "the priest of God Most High" (Heb. 7:1).

Later on in the Bible, we learn that this priest-king, Melchizedek, is a type or picture of the Lord Jesus Christ. The priest served Abraham bread and wine, and Abraham gave him "a tenth of everything" (Gen. 14:20).

What a high that must have been! You conquer an alliance of four armies with a bunch of shepherds, you stand strong as a stone wall against an evil king, and you get a blessing and a banquet from the "priest of God Most High."

That had to be just a little bit gratifying.

In terms of Abraham experiencing Life², this had to be one of the most amazing of breakthrough moments. He would have never experienced anything close to the adventures, perils, and triumphs if he had ignored God's call and wiled away his life in "good old Ur."

But Abraham had obeyed the voice from heaven, taken the risk, paid the price, and placed his whole future in God's hands. Now he was certainly experiencing life on a higher—and certainly more interesting!—level.

But Abram didn't stay put at that new level of living very long.

"AFTER THIS...."

After this, the word of the Lord came to Abram in a vision: "Do not be afraid, Abram. I am your shield, your very great reward."

—GENESIS 15:1

"After this."

Those two words caught my attention as I read Genesis 15. I believe every word in the Bible is there for a reason. What is the Holy Spirit trying to tell us with those two pivotal words?

Perhaps "after this" indicates a turn signal, a warning light.

I flew to North Carolina earlier this week, and we experienced some strong turbulence at several points in the flight. I noticed that early in the turbulence process a little bell would come on, and then the pilot would inform us that we would be in rough air for a while, so we should keep our seatbelts fastened.

Maybe Abraham's "after this" was like that telltale bell: get ready for a turn of events, get ready for some turbulence.

Linda and I were flying on a commuter plane recently, and couldn't help tuning in to an interesting conversation between two ladies in front of us. One of them was saying, "I have a friend who's a flight attendant for Alaska Airlines. Three years ago she was on the crew of a flight originating in Alaska and bound for Seattle. Somewhere in the midst of the flight, without warning, they hit a thousand foot air pocket. The plane turned upside down and dropped like a stone for a thousand feet. After what must have seemed like an eternity to the people on board, the plane hit the bottom of the pocket, leveled out, and landed safely at SeaTac."

It reminds me of what Jesus told us about life on this planet: "In this world you will have trouble" (John 16:33). Another way to say that might be, "In this world you will have air pockets." In other words, we're going to have some downdrafts. Some little—just enough to make us a little unsettled and queasy—and some very large and terrifying.

And then came "after this." After what? After these amazing triumphs and the elation of walking in what Jesus would call "more and better life."

The transition between Genesis 14 and 15 must have been such an encounter with turbulence for Abraham. In the fourteenth chapter, it's easy to see that the man from Ur had experienced a good strong taste of Life². It was more than a concept or theory. He was living it, and God was both blessing him and causing him to be a blessing to others.

ABRAHAM'S FEAR FACTOR

When you turn the page to Genesis 15, it looks like the good times were going to keep on rolling for Abraham: "After this, the word of the LORD came to Abram in a vision: 'Do not be afraid, Abram. I am your shield, your very great reward.'"

That sounds like a pretty strong word of encouragement to me. But why does the Lord say, "Abram, don't be afraid"?

Because, in that moment, Abraham must have been gripped by fear. There are 366 "fear nots" in the Bible—one for every day of the year plus leap year. And in most of them, the Lord or His angels are seeking to comfort men and women who are absolutely terrified by their circumstances in life.

What was the cause of Abraham's fear? Maybe you can identify with this: He felt as though life was passing him by. In particular, he saw that he was getting older and older, and that he and Sarah (then known as "Sarai") still had no children. He replied to the Lord, "What can you give me since I remain childless?" (Gen. 15:2).

His very name at that time, Abram, "father of many," seemed like a mockery to him. "Lord, what can You give me? I'm 90 years old. My wife and I are well past childbearing years. You promised us a child, and we've waited and waited. It's just not happening, and that makes me afraid."

Abraham, who at age 90 had led a daring commando raid against four allied kingdoms, sending enemy soldiers running for their lives, now found himself in a personal downdraft that almost felt like a freefall.

Sometimes the prospect of facing a whole army is less frightening than facing our own doubts, by ourselves, in the dark. Abraham had staked his whole life on God. And was God now letting him down? Did God truly care about him?

Perhaps you've been in a spot like that. You charged into the Christian life staking your life and your eternity on Jesus, and now, where is He? I don't know. This just isn't working for me.

I'm afraid I'm not going to make it. I doubt that I can. I'm finding it harder and harder to believe that God really cares.

We are a fearful people. Afraid of death. Afraid of accidents. Afraid of loneliness. Afraid of failure. I hear it all the time as a pastor. People will say to me, "I'm afraid I'm going to fail. I can't seem to live this Christian life. I keep failing God."

I recently had a brother come up to me after one of our services. "Pastor," he said, "I've just got to tell you. I was clean for ninety days, then I blew it Friday on some meth. I didn't mean to. I didn't want to. I just went out with some friends for a couple of beers and then...."

I could see the fear in his eyes. He didn't want to be hooked. He didn't want to trash his life. He didn't want to fail the Lord. And he was just appalled by what he had done.

"You know what?" I told him. "You're doing the right thing. You're here, in church. And you're telling me about this and making yourself accountable. We're going to get some people around you, and you're going to get free of this."

Perhaps the "after this" in verse 1 indicates not only a turn of events in Abram's life, but an indication that what came "before this" caused his "after this" doubts.

The point is, Abraham didn't have a perfect track record. When famine came to the land of Canaan, he immediately tucked tail and ran down to Egypt. Check out the account; there is no indication he even asked God about this crucial move. Egypt was where he tried to pawn his wife off as his sister, and she almost ended up as one of Pharaoh's concubines. It certainly wasn't the strongest point on his resume.

Perhaps Abraham's doubt that God would actually give him a son of promise was based on self-doubt. Perhaps his fear, addressed by God, was actually fear of failure, rooted in a review of his much-less-than-perfect past.

Do you ever feel like God surely must feel the need to pare back on His promises because of your poor performance? Hear the heart of the Lord toward His sometimes-failing servant: "Don't be afraid, Abraham. I am your shield, your very great reward. It's not about who you are, it's about who I am. It's not about your poor performance, it's about My amazing grace."

We all face those times of fear and doubt and regret—no matter how close our relationship with the Lord has been. The issue isn't avoiding the air pockets in life, the issue is leveling out the plane after you've gone through them. The issue is getting back on your feet again.

I've found that pursuing Life^2 is a process. There's no such thing as Life^2 autopilot. It's not a once-and-for-all thing, no matter what anyone tells you. And though the patriarch Abraham experienced some high and exalted moments in his long walk with God, he certainly had those times when it was all he could do to keep from doing a face-plant. In Genesis 15, we see him starting to lose his grip on his former faith.

There are so many things that can pull us down. Jesus said so in the very same breath where He uttered, "I have come that they may have life, and have it to the full." He prefaced those words with the reminder that "the thief comes only to steal and kill and destroy" (John 10:10).

You have an enemy—thief, serial killer, destroyer—who wants to keep you from a breakthrough in your walk with Christ. If you find yourself standing at the trailhead of a new life pathway, he'll try to turn you away before you get three steps down the trail.

AMBUSH ON THE TRAIL

When my daughter Christin was eleven years old, I took her on a hike with me up in the Cascade mountain range. We were climbing up the mountain on a game trail I'd come across weeks earlier.

It was a special, secret place, and we didn't see another person all day. About noon, I saw a marshy lake a half mile or so off the trail. I'm always scouting for elk, and elk-like marshes, so I talked Christin into following me over there for a look.

When we got to the lake, we decided to walk out on a little peninsula. I stepped over a dead log on the game trail and headed on.

Suddenly Christin screamed. "Dad! Dad! Help!"

I looked back to see her surrounded by yellow jackets. She had stepped on a yellow jacket nest.

"Run!" I said. I ran back to her and grabbed her hand. By the time we reached safety, she had been stung four times. Her face and arm began to swell up, and we hurried down the mountain to get some medical help. That was one adventure she will never forget.

That's the way it can be with our life in Christ. We come at last to a trailhead and a walk into the wilderness that promises sights and experiences beyond anything we've known before. But our desire to go higher, to leave the familiar and explore new territory, stirs up hell's hornet nest.

Jesus said, "I saw Satan fall like lightning from heaven" (Luke 10:18), and now the enemy wants to take everyone down with him that he can possibly take down.

Personal failures pull us down. Gloomy feelings pull us down. Some of us battle with our emotions. We look out on the horizon of our lives and it seems gloomy. We begin to lose our dreams. And one morning we get out of bed and just feel afraid.

Three years ago, two of our key leaders left our church without the blessing of the elders and pastors, and started churches in Bend. Several hundred people went with one of the leaders, and several dozen people went with the other leader.

To tell the truth, it felt like a swift punch in the stomach, and it pulled me down into depression. The enemy seemed to put his magnifying glass on my shortcomings. "If you had done better at this…if you weren't so poor at this, they wouldn't have left."

For several months, every Monday morning brought fresh thoughts of aborting the dream God gave me for our church and our city. I wanted to give up on the dream, give up on myself.

That's where Abraham was. From where he stood, the future looked pretty dismal. He and the Mrs. had no children. And remembering that God's promise was supposed to come to him through a miracle child, Abraham had to wonder about that promise—and maybe about God Himself.

Abraham found himself gripped by fear and despair. Even when God Himself appeared to him with a personal promise, the patriarch couldn't shake the mantle of gloom.

> But Abram said, "O Sovereign Lord, what can you give me since I remain childless and the one who will inherit my estate is Eliezer of Damascus?" And Abram said, "You have given me no children; so a servant in my household will be my heir."
>
> —GENESIS 15:2–3

There are times in our lives when we feel so drained, so depressed, so low, so beaten down by our circumstances that even a visitation from God can't pull us through.

Once you allow the darkness of your emotions or circumstances to blind your spiritual eyes and close your spiritual ears, you could even miss God Himself saying to you, "Don't be afraid...I am your shield, your very great reward" (v. 1).

Abraham had a hard time hearing and responding to this word because he was busy watching a movie of his past projected onto the screen of his future. He was saying to himself, "I'm old, and I'm never going to have a child. It's not going to happen." Be careful about assuming your future will simply be a rerun of your past! We serve an infinitely creative, all-powerful God who is full of surprises and loves us more than we can imagine. When you spend most of your time looking backward, or staring at your present situation, Life² looks impossible.

After God promises Abraham (once again) a son and a homeland, the discouraged man replies, "O Sovereign LORD, how can I know that I will gain possession of it?" (v. 8).

You may find yourself dealing with a similar reaction as you read these pages. "How can I know there really is a Life²? How do I know this isn't so much charismatic happy-talk? How can I know that it can actually happen for me?"

Maybe when you became a follower of Christ, when you were baptized, when you were filled with the Holy Spirit, someone told you, "That's it. You're on top. There won't be any more problems." Well, they lied to you because you can't and you won't stay on top from here to heaven. If there was a perfect world and we were perfect people, that would be possible, but neither of those things is true.

Apparently, the Alaska flight attendant who experienced the thousand-foot air pocket quit her job as soon as the plane landed, went into therapy, and has never stepped foot inside an airplane again.

The same can be true of you and me. We become afraid to fly. Afraid to hope. Afraid to dream. We had those hopes and dreams at one time, but then we hit such a huge air pocket and fell so far that we don't even want to think about climbing back into life at a higher level. We say, "I don't reach for the clouds again, because I'll probably fall just like the last time. I don't even want to hope. I don't even want to try. I'm afraid."

This isn't "life squared," this is life scared.

That's where Abraham was. And he was frightened to the point that God couldn't even speak to him about his future until He had calmed the man down a little.

Abraham said to God in verse 3: "You have given me no children; so a servant in my household will be my heir." In other words, I know what You've promised. Believe me, I have rehearsed those promises a thousand times as I've walked along the way or tossed and turned in my tent at night, unable to sleep. I know what You have said, but maybe I didn't get it right, because it just doesn't seem to be working.

We could say the same thing about Life². "Jesus, I know that You promised life on a higher level. I know that the Bible keeps pointing to something more, something better out there, but it's just not working for me. It's not happening in my life, and I'm giving up hope."

All God wants you to do is be honest with Him, and ask Him to help you. He doesn't want you to pretend and put on a plastic smile or fake some kind of Spirit-filled excitement. He wants you to be real with Him.

Did God reprimand Abraham for expressing his fears? Not at all. The Lord simply set the record straight—and renewed His promise of a miracle:

> Then the word of the Lord came to him: "This man will not be your heir, but a son coming from your own body will be your heir."
>
> —Genesis 15:4

We need to give God the chance to set the record straight. We need to pour the contents of our heart out before Him, and let Him sort it out. He will, my friend, He will. David wrote, "When my spirit was overwhelmed within me, then You knew my path" (Ps. 142:3, NKJV). And so it is for you at this very moment. No matter how overwhelmed you might feel, God knows your path, and He will gently guide you as you place your full trust in Him.

Night Light

Why does God allow these low tides in our lives? Ultimately, only He knows. But it may very well be He wants to show you something wonderful that you could have never seen in the brightness of daylight. Something that shows up best on a dark night.

When Abraham came to his own dark place of doubt and fear, God was there, shining so much brighter than His glorious handiwork in the heavens. And then God spoke to him, "The word of the Lord came to Abram in a vision" (Gen. 15:1).

This is exactly what you and I need in those deep-down-in-the-canyon times. We need a word from the Lord. We need to hear God's voice. I can put up with a lot—grief, fear, weariness, perplexity, pain—if I can hear God speak to me in the midst of it. And the Lord was saying to His downcast servant, "I will do what I said I would do in your life, son. You need to believe Me and wait on Me, because it will be worth it."

Genesis 15:5 is one of those verses in a narrative portion of Scripture that I've probably read a thousand times. But on the thousand-and-first time, it hit me with such force it almost brought me to tears.

> He took him outside and said, "Look up at the heavens and count the stars—if indeed you can count them." Then he said to him, "So shall your offspring be."

Who took whom outside? God took Abraham. Apparently, this conversation had been going on inside Abraham's tent. But then God wanted a change of scene. How did He do it? How did He take Abraham out under the open sky? I like to think it was like an arm around the man's shoulder. Or maybe hand in hand.

What time of day was it? It was night—deep, dark, and still.

As I reflect on this, it seems to me God was saying something like this to Abraham: "I know these have been hard days for you. I know you feel like you're right on the ragged edge of your endurance. I know you're down at heart. Tell you what...why don't you and I take a walk? Let's just go for a little stroll and we'll talk some more. I have something I want to show you."

There was no "light pollution" in Abraham's day. No smog. No porch lights or head lights or street lights. No horizon-illuminating glow from a distant city. When this story transpired, the world was very young. Night was really night, and stars were really stars. What a panorama it must have been as God and His friend (see Isaiah 41:8) lifted that tent flap and walked out into the desert night.

Stars shine all the time, of course, if we could see them. But we can't see them at all in the light of day. And even at night in a big city, the stars may be only a few dim points of light. But out in the wilderness under a midnight sky, they sparkle like diamonds against black velvet.

There are truths and insights, I believe, that God wants to reveal to each one of us. But some can only be seen at night. There may be lessons—wondrous glimpses into our future—that we can only see after the light of day fades, and the stars come out one by one. Yes, the night hours of life can be frightening. Life certainly changes when we hit bottom, and find ourselves in deep emotional, physical, or spiritual darkness.

But something good can happen in the night.

If you go for a walk with God.

A few months after those two key leaders and their followers left our church, leaving us a church family in emotional shock, I was sitting in my office at the church trying to bolster the courage to handle the tasks at hand when I heard the Spirit whisper to my soul, "Walk out to your car with Me, and go up on Awbrey Butte."

Our church campus is at the base of that largest butte in town. I thought, "This seems silly, but I need to obey what I believe to be the Lord's voice."

I drove up on the butte, got out of my car, and looked down on the church campus. God spoke inaudibly but indelibly to me at that point: "See that road running in front of the church. I'm going to pack that road with cars coming to Westside Church. In those cars will be people who are considering suicide. They will receive help and hope at Westside, and they will be shining lights to others who feel helpless and hopeless. In those cars will be couples who are considering divorce. I will breathe new life into their souls and their marriage at Westside. They will be beacons of My grace and power to other couples who feel their marriage is about to crash on rocky shoals. I am going to entrust to you three people for every person that left."

In the last two years, I've been amazed at the ways God has been bringing people to our church. Last Easter we had a thirty-minute traffic jam, with cars backed up for half a mile, trying to get into the Westside driveway for our fourth Easter service. A few months ago, a young man walked into one of our staff meetings, and our youth pastor, Corey, went to talk with him. He told Corey that he was driving by the church and he heard a voice in his heart that said, "You need to drive in there and find God." Corey led him across the line of faith, and God added an exponent to his life starting that very moment.

Your clearest reference point, your greatest revelation, may come to you in your darkest night.

Think about it. You don't pursue light unless you're really in the dark. You don't seek directions unless you're lost. You don't drink deeply unless you're very thirsty. And maybe we only discover a companionship like no other when we feel lonely and find ourselves longing for the friendship of God. That's how it was for Abraham. God confirmed His promise to him in the night, and He did it in a way He could have never done in broad daylight.

God gave Abraham a picture that night—a glorious, unforgettable picture to go along with a renewed promise. And Abraham learned something very important—God works the night shift.[3]

(This is the title of a wonderful book by my friend, Dr. Ron Mehl, now with Jesus in a place where it will never be dark again.)

And He knows all about our heartaches and down times. Psalm 103 says:

> The Lord is like a father to his children, tender and compassionate to those who fear him. For he understands how weak we are; he knows we are only dust.
>
> —PSALM 103:13–14, NLT

Paul contributes these encouraging words:

> There has never been the slightest doubt in my mind that the God who started this great work in you would keep at it and bring it to a flourishing finish on the very day Christ Jesus appears.
>
> —PHILIPPIANS 1:6, THE MESSAGE

We can be failing, we can be fearful, but because of God's great love and compassion, He will never leave us. He is committed to finish what He started in us.

High or low.
Night or day.
Come what may.

CHAPTER 3

OVERCOMING GRAVITY

What keeps Christ-followers from walking in the more-and-better life He promised us?

About five years ago, I got into a private plane with Tom, a pilot I knew, and flew to Eastern Oregon to scout out some elk hunting territory. How was I to know that Tom was a frustrated aerobatic daredevil?

I really don't know what I'd been expecting when we walked up to the plane on the runway at our little Bend airport. But it was certainly something more substantial than this. This plane looked like a toy—so tiny I could hardly believe my eyes.

"Tom? You don't mean we're going up in this thing, do you?"

My pilot just smiled and escorted me to my designated seat, just behind his. When we were buckled in, Tom closed the little hatch over our heads. Honestly, the picture I had in my mind at that moment was the little clear-plastic inverted container that goes on top of a popcorn popper. It looked about that sturdy.

After we were airborne, it quickly heated up inside that little popcorn popper. With the warmth and the bumpy air, I began to feel woozy.

Suddenly, my seatbelt felt confining. I unhooked it.

Immediately I felt better, and relaxed for a minute or two. But then I started to worry a little. What if we hit an air pocket or something? I told myself I'd probably better hook that thing. I fastened it around my waist, but loosely, so it wouldn't constrict my rebellious stomach.

In what seemed like mere moments after I snapped in again, my whole world suddenly turned upside down. Tom had decided, without consulting me, to flip the plane over and fly upside down for awhile.

If I had left my seatbelt unhooked, I can tell you, we wouldn't be having this conversation. I would have gone right through that popcorn popper cover—without a parachute! There's no way that frail little thing could have held my weight.

I was hanging from the loose seatbelt—but passionately thanking God for it. As soon as I got my breath back, I yelled at Tom, "Turn this sucker right-side up!"

Even if we never climb into a frail little aircraft with an acrobatic pilot, our lives will have ups and downs aplenty. Sometimes when it feels like we're flying upside down or doing loopty-loops, we long for a little security. In this chapter we'll see how God gave Abraham a safety belt in a down time of his life. It came in the form of a covenant, a binding agreement with His friend. (See Isaiah 41:8.)

SLEEPLESS IN CANAAN

As we saw in the previous chapter, Abraham had reached a stretch of road in his long pilgrimage where he felt beset by fear and anxiety. Was life passing him by? Had God forgotten about his promise of a son and heir? Who would end up inheriting all he had? A household servant?

As we saw, God took Abraham out under the night sky and said, "Look up into the heavens and count the stars if you can. Your descendants will be like that—too many to count!" (See Genesis 15:5.)

God said to him, "Abraham, look up!"

It seems evident from the text that prior to this encounter, Abraham had been doing a lot of looking down. The thought that God would make a promise to him and then seemingly not follow through had him feeling pretty low.

We tend to follow our face, don't we? If we're looking up, that's the direction our life tends to head. And if we persist in looking down, we'll slide into discouragement, depression, or worse. I don't know where I heard this not-so-elegant expression, but it has come back to me many times: Stinkin' thinkin' will leave you sinkin'.

You need to use your faith muscles—and so do I. They're right there at the corners of your mouth. When your heart is lifted to God in faith, those faith muscles in your face tend to lift up a smile on your face. And your life will usually follow the direction of your chin!

The gravity of everyday living will wear you down if you let it. Give it free reign and it will pull your countenance down, and then the direction of your eyes will fall, and there's no telling what will fall after that.

So the fact is, your life may not look up until you do.

Abraham, by faith, experienced that lift in the presence of God. The text says, "Abram believed the LORD, and he [the Lord] credited it to him as righteousness" (Gen. 15:6).

In that wonderful moment Abraham was airborne, flying by faith. By following the Lord's gaze and seeing things from His perspective, he had conquered gravity.

It could have lasted for a long, long time.

But it didn't. All too soon, Abraham turned his gaze from those stars and began a downhill slide.

LONGING FOR LIFE

Abraham's wife, Sarah, hadn't experienced that walk under the stars, and her heart was still filled with anxiety. But instead of countering Sarah's discouragement and fears with his renewed faith, Abraham relapsed into his old limited perspective.

But Sarai, Abram's wife, had no children. So Sarai took her servant, an Egyptian woman named Hagar, and gave her to Abram so she could bear his children. "The LORD has kept me from having any children" (Gen. 16:2).

Sarai said to Abram:

> "Go and sleep with my servant. Perhaps I can have children through her." And Abram agreed….So Sarai, Abram's wife, took Hagar the Egyptian servant and gave her to Abram as a wife….So Hagar gave Abram a son, and Abram named him Ishmael.
>
> —GENESIS 16:2–3, 15, NLT

And so you have the birth of the Arabic people, and Mid-East turmoil right down to the present day.

Abraham and Sarah were longing for new life in their family, and God is all about life. He is pro-life in the broadest sense, because He is a prolific God and the God of prolific living. For most of us living in the western world, prolific means piling up money and possessions, having a nice house, working at a good job, driving the right car, and taking vacations in beautiful places.

To the eastern mind, prolific means having kids.

It was just about the most important thing in life to them. With the birth of a baby, they could look at each other and say, "Now this is living. This is what it's all about."

In the theme verse for this book, John 10:10, Jesus said, "I came so that they can have more and better life" (THE MESSAGE).

What is more and better life to you? What does prolific life mean to you? What would make you say, "Now this is living!" (For some reason I have a mental picture here of a misty dawn on the slope of a mountain in Eastern Oregon, calling a bull elk.)

The fact is, God offers life at a higher level. That may not mean vacations and bull elk, but it does mean "more and better life" in your walk with Him. But at this point in the story, Abraham and Sarah have turned from the promise of God to seek life on their own terms. Yes, they're having a child, as God had promised. But rather than waiting for His provision, they're doing it on their own.

What is it that keeps pulling us down, time after time, so that we fall off the mountain of Life[2] and go back to living in the bottom of the valley?

If you have wrestled with that question (and who hasn't), don't feel alone in the struggle. Even the apostle Paul felt the strong effects of gravity.

THE TROUBLE WITH GRAVITY

What's the trouble with gravity? It never goes away!

In Romans 7, Paul penned these unforgettable words:

> So I find this law at work: When I want to do good, evil is
> right there with me. For in my inner being I delight in God's
> law; but I see another law at work in the members of my
> body, waging war against the law of my mind and making
> me a prisoner of the law of sin at work within my members.
> What a wretched man I am! Who will rescue me from this
> body of death?
>
> —ROMANS 7:21–25

Can you relate to those words? Sometimes it seems like Paul
has been looking over my shoulder as I write in my journal! I want
to live well for the Lord, but I end up doing less than I wanted.
I really desire to please God and do what's right—"I delight in
God's law"—but so often I end up doing what's wrong.

"What a wretched man I am. Who will rescue me from this
body of death?"

What keeps dragging us down? Why do we always seem to be
swimming in concrete boots? Even Paul admitted that though
he believed in the resurrection of Jesus, he couldn't seem to get
off the ground sometimes. The Bible says we're afflicted with
"the body of death," and that phrase has some rather gruesome
origins. In the Roman culture, if you murdered someone and
they caught you absolutely red-handed, they had a legal system
that sometimes would chain the corpse to the murderer—arm to
arm, leg to leg, waist to waist. And they'd let the corpse rot on the
back of the killer. (I think I would prefer lethal injection.)

Paul uses that graphic picture to describe how believers struggle all their lives with the downward pull of our flesh—our old, sinful nature. I sometimes call it my "BC" self, a darker side that tries to trip me up and pull me down. The dead part of me is chained to the living part of me! So the question is: How then do we live life at a higher level—and stay airborne longer and longer? The answer is in the first verse of chapter 8: "Therefore, there is now no condemnation for those who are in Christ Jesus."

Because of Christ Jesus, Paul tells us, the law of the spirit of life sets us free from the law of sin and death.

So we're faced with two laws as believers. We have the law of gravity and the law of aerodynamics. You can deny them, but they're there. There's a law of the spirit of life, and there's a law of sin and death.

The Bible says:

> Those who live according to the sinful nature have their minds set on what that nature desires; but those who live in accordance with the Spirit have their minds set on what the Spirit desires. The mind of the sinful person is death, but the mind controlled by the Spirit is life.
>
> —ROMANS 8:5

Just because you get in a plane and experience aerodynamics lifting you up into the wide blue sky, doesn't mean that there is no gravity. If you open the door and jump out, where are you going? Nowhere but down!

So, from the time you step out of the airplane until the time you begin freefall, that's about how long you last when you try to fly on your own.

DEFYING THE LAW OF GRAVITY

The book of Isaiah tells us that "those who hope in the LORD will renew their strength. They will soar on wings like eagles" (Isa. 40:31).

Think about how an airplane soars. As the plane moves forward, the movement of the wind over the top of the wings creates a vacuum, pulling the whole aircraft higher and higher.

There's a spiritual truth like that, too. When God speaks to us and we move toward what He's saying, it creates an uplift that can overcome gravity. The law of gravity doesn't go away, but it is overruled by the law of aerodynamics.

After I had been a Christian for two years, I remember sitting in church one Sunday listening to the pastor talk about life on a higher level, just as I've spoken of in the pages of this book. I'd been trying to walk with God, but I felt terribly discouraged about the results. Sometimes I would enjoy that exhilarating sense of aliveness and the presence of God, and at other times I'd fall back into my old, shabby ways.

I remember silently telling the Lord, I quit. I can't do this. God, I love You, but I can't do this Christian thing. It's way too hard for me. I can't be a Christian. And I heard this little voice that spoke inside my heart and said, "Good! Let Me do it! Let Me do it in and through you."

Now maybe you've heard that sort of thing before, but I hadn't. It was a whole new concept to me that it might be God's power and not just my diligence and effort that would allow me to rise to a higher level.

There's only one person who has fully lived the Christian life: Jesus Christ. That's why we call it the CHRISTian life. We live it to different degrees, but only He has fully lived up to God's standards—pure, righteous, and utterly consistent.

That's why Romans 8:1 says that there is no condemnation if you are in Christ Jesus. If you are in the airplane, you can supersede the law of gravity and fly just about as high as you like. If you are in Christ Jesus, you can supersede the law of sin and death and experience Life[2].

Trying to fly high in Christ on your own efforts makes about as much sense as jogging down a runway flapping your arms. You'll get some aerobic exercise and work up a sweat, but your feet will never leave the ground.

I like the way the biblical writer says it in the book of Hebrews: "So come on, let's leave the preschool fingerpainting exercises on Christ and get on with the grand work of art. Grow up in Christ...turning your back on 'salvation by self-help' and turning in trust toward God....There's so much more. Let's get on with it!" (Heb. 6:1–3, THE MESSAGE).

When you get up on Monday morning—or any morning, for that matter—you will always be faced with those same two spiritual laws: the law of sin and death, and the law of life in Christ Jesus.

Which law wins? It's your choice. As long as you remain in Christ, you remain in Life[2].

In John 15:4, Jesus spoke three of the most significant words any believer could ever hear and heed: "Remain in me."

Other translations say, "Abide in me" (KJV). One paraphrase puts it like this: "Take care to live in me" (TLB).

It's all the same idea, speaking of a living, functional union between Jesus Christ and His followers. He went on to say:

"Remain in me, and I will remain in you. No branch can bear fruit by itself; it must remain in the vine. Neither can you bear fruit unless you remain in me. I am the vine; you are the branches. If a man remains in me and I in him, he will bear much fruit; apart from me you can do nothing."

—JOHN 15:4–5

The very life flow of Jesus Christ fills us, energizes us, sustains us, and lifts us as we consciously remain in Him, walking moment by moment in His Holy Spirit.

CONTINUAL LIFT

Have you heard the voice of God this week, as you've opened the pages of His Word and taken time to be alone with Him? When we receive the Words of God, take it into our lives, and act on it, it becomes the life of Christ in us. And that's the continual lift that overrules the forces that would drag us down, down, down, giving us aerodynamic lift into the bright blue skies of Life².

The more you live this way, the more you will escape the law of gravity. That's why Jesus said that those who have will have even more, and those who have not and don't use what they have will end up with nothing. (See Matthew 25:25–29.) They'll never really get off the ground.

Think about how a rocket takes off from Cape Canaveral. You can hear the thunder of the thrusters and see the mighty flames from miles away. It takes a lot of fuel to get past the gravitational pull of earth. It also takes a lot of fuel to get past the gravitational pull of this selfish world, and to live a Christ-like, selfless life. Huge amounts of fuel!

What is the fuel? It is the Word of God brought to us by the Spirit of God, breaking us free from the ceaseless downward pull and allowing us to soar.

Back in John 15, where Jesus spoke about the prolific life available for those who remain in Him, He also made a blunt point about self-effort: "Apart from me," He said, "you can do nothing."

> How much?
> Nothing.
> Maybe just a little bit?
> No, nothing at all.

I meet believers all the time who don't really believe that. They'll say something like this: "Yes, it's been awhile since I really walked with God, but I've still been able to accomplish some things. I'm raising my kids. I make my mortgage. I have my occupation and do a good job at it. That's something, isn't it?"

It may seem like something in the moment, but ultimately, the Bible tells us, it will amount to nothing. If it was done outside the life of Jesus Christ, separate from Him, it will add up to precisely zero.

Jesus has been to the future and back, and He knows about that great climactic fire that will engulf everything that's not eternal. In fact, the only things that will last are the things which God Himself does.

At one point in his life, Abraham might have said, "You didn't tell me to make love to Hagar and father a baby on my own. But I did it. Sarah and I took matters into our own hands, and we gained a son. How can You say that's nothing? Isn't that proof that I can do at least something?"

Yes, Abraham did something. But it amounted to nothing and less than nothing. The boy's name was Ishmael. *El* means "God" and *shamah* means "to hear with intelligence." So what Abraham did with Hagar was on the basis of his own reason, not on the basis of revelation. He did it on the basis of human desire, not on the basis of God's Word.

Thank you, Abraham, for the Mid-East conflict!

Abraham's actions not only made his own life difficult, but four thousand years later his ancestors in Israel are still dealing with the consequences. And that's what happens when we operate on the basis of our reason and not God's Word.

UPDRAFTS AND DOWNDRAFTS

When you hear God's Word and obey it, when you seek to live by what God has shown you, just think of an airplane lifting off a runway and making a steep climb. When we act on what God says to us, He will speak more, giving us more to do, more of His words, more of Himself.

And then we'll say, "This is living. This is good!"

The life-lift we experience as we exercise our faith will lift up our heads and lift up a smile on our faces. It won't be a pasted-on smile, or something forced. You don't have to buy a pogo-stick to get airborne. You catch the updraft of God's life and "soar on wings like eagles" (Isa. 40:31).

Can it get even better? Yes, tomorrow can be even better than today. Gravity will never go away, but neither will the power of God as we choose to live in it.

You say, "But I keep hitting these air pockets—these huge downdrafts. After worship and being with God's people on Sunday, I'm flying high. But by Monday noon—after I've encountered all the cursing, backbiting, and negativity at work—I feel myself losing altitude. I lose that sense of God's presence in my life. How can I stay airborne?"

What follows in Genesis 15 is one of the most mysterious, most moving scenes I've ever encountered in Scripture.

Going back to Abraham's encounter with the Lord, it seems as though he still felt a little queasy about the conversation:

> [God] also said to him, "I am the Lord, who brought you out of Ur of the Chaldeans to give you this land to take possession of it." But Abram said, "O Sovereign Lord, how can I know that I will gain possession of it?"
>
> —GENESIS 15:7–8

God had already taken a walk under the stars with Abraham, reaffirming His promises, and Abraham had believed the word of the Lord. But this thing about possessing the land? Why, he was little more than an alien in Canaan, and at that point, he really didn't own a single inch of the land. What did God mean? How would this work?

And I think we ask something similar about Life^2. Lord, I've struggled for so long to get off the ground and stay off the ground. You've held out the promise of more and better life, but, how does it work? How can I know it will work for me? How can I live this life?

What the Lord did at that point so amazes me. He didn't have to answer Abraham at all! He had already given Him a promise, restating it again and again. But how the Lord loved Abraham! And how He loves you and me. He will go the extra mile—and infinitely further—to answer a seeking heart.

So the Lord said to him, "Bring me a heifer, a goat and a ram, each three years old, along with a dove and a young pigeon." Abram brought all these to him, cut them in two and arranged the halves opposite each other; the birds, however, he did not cut in half.

—GENESIS 15: 9–10

This was a ceremony that Abraham knew well. In the Mid-East, when two parties wanted to make a solemn covenant, they would do just as the Lord commanded Abraham to do—dividing these animals, and creating a bloody path between the halves. Both parties would then pass through the broken animals, and that's how they notarized or made a legal contract. By participating in this ceremony, you were in essence saying, "We have made an agreement, and this agreement will be broken over my dead body. It will not happen."

God did that with Abraham.

God Himself walked through the broken pieces, while Abraham lay on the turf, semi-conscious. This was a staggering thing, when you think about it. The Almighty, Eternal, God of the Universe walked through the pieces, the broken bodies, the shed blood, saying in essence, "This agreement will be broken over My dead body."

Look at verse 18: "And on that day, the LORD made a covenant with Abram." God committed Himself to a binding agreement so that Abraham's heart could be at rest. No matter what happened, He knew God would come through. The land would belong to his descendants, though not a one of them had been born yet.

Broken body? Shed blood?

Yes, it reminds us of Jesus and the "new covenant" made "in His blood" (Luke 22:20). In another solemn ceremony—shot through with tenderness—Jesus pronounced the terms of a new covenant: "Then he took the cup, gave thanks and offered it to them, saying, 'Drink from it, all of you. This is my blood of the covenant, which is poured out for many for the forgiveness of sins'" (Matt. 26:27–28).

His body would be broken. His blood would be shed. His eleven remaining disciples would abandon Him, fleeing to save their own skins. But Jesus would stick with them through the darkest night anyone has ever faced. Even though they had forsaken Him, He would never leave nor forsake them. (See Hebrews 13:5.) He had made a covenant with them: "Over my dead body."

Every time we take communion, the bread and the cup, we remember that Jesus sealed a covenant with us, and not only with words. The same Israelite soil that soaked up the blood of Abraham's covenant ceremony soaked up Jesus' blood as well. We remember that Jesus died for us. That He will never abandon us or leave as orphans. And that we are safe as long as we are in Him.

If you received Christ and entered into covenant life with God, you're buckled in. He has saved you with His promise, and He sustains you with His promise. He will take you through the ups and downs and keep your airplane in the air, because He loves you and has committed Himself to you.

He wants to do forever with you. He wants to do today with you, too.

He wants to be real to you, to speak to you, and have you speak to Him, becoming nothing less than your best friend.

"Be strong and courageous. Do not be afraid…for the LORD your God goes with you; he will never leave you nor forsake you" (Deut. 31:6).

Don't you love that? He will never leave you or forsake you. If you're buckled in, you're going to be safe. You're not going to be flawless, but you'll be safe as long as you're in Christ.

CHAPTER 4

DEATH GRIP

Taking hold of the life we've always wanted means releasing our grip on the life we've always known.

Every young boy craves adventure, and growing up near Newberg, Oregon, I had the run of miles of trails through the woods along Chehalem Creek and the banks of the wide Willamette River.

I remember taking my fishing pole down to the creek one sunny Saturday morning in May. I loved to fish the creek early in the morning because I would see squirrels, ducks, deer, geese—wildlife in abundance.

I was walking along the north bank of the creek about 200 yards up from where it ran into the Willamette River when I came across a Mallard hen. Just for fun, I started to run at the hen, and she ran off, flapping her wings but barely clearing the ground. She appeared to be wounded. I was just about to take chase when out of the corner of my eye I caught a glimpse of several little brown ducklings to my left running for cover. Mama was only pretending to be wounded, trying to distract me from her little ones.

I remember jogging down a path along the creek one Saturday morning and surprising a mother duck and her ducklings. The hen flapped off into the water like she was wounded, trying to distract me from her little ones. But I knew that trick, and didn't fall for it. Most of the ducklings scurried toward the water, but one ran in a panic the wrong direction, and tried to hide under some fallen leaves.

I caught it and took it home.

When I showed my prize to my dad, however, he winced and shook his head. "That's not a good thing, son."

"But Dad," I protested, "I was just trying to help. I thought it might be lost. I thought it might die if I didn't do something."

Dad put an arm on my shoulder. "The mother and the duckling would have found each other, Kenny. But now that baby duck will die."

How do dads just know stuff like that? He was so sure the duckling couldn't live away from its mother and the water. But that's not what I wanted to hear. I wanted to show him I could take care of the little duck and make a pet out of it. Cutting down a cardboard box I found in the garage, I made a warm nest for it, and tried to feed it delicacies I thought ducklings might like to eat.

But Dad was right after all. In spite of hovering over that little bird all day, in spite of all my efforts, care, and good intentions, the little duckling didn't live out the night. Trying to help it, trying to hold onto that little life for my own, I killed it.

It's funny how the mind works sometimes. Just recently, as I was thinking through this chapter, that poignant childhood memory came back to me, reminding me of something I never want to forget: It's what happens when we cling to life on our own terms.

In fact, it just doesn't work. If you take a firm grip on life according to your own designs and desires, you'll kill it. It will become a death grip, and what you want so much to live will simply die.

Jesus said it clearly, "For whoever wants to save his life will lose it, but whoever loses his life for me and for the gospel will save it" (Mark 8:35). It's something of a twist on the old childhood saying: "Finders, keepers; losers, weepers." In the spiritual realm, its finders, losers; losers, keepers.

Abraham and Sarah had to learn that Life² lesson, and as with so many vital and valuable truths, the learning didn't come easy. They had to experience it the hard way.

WHOSE "I WILL ..."?

When God had said to Abraham, "Leave your country, your people and your father's household and go to the land I will show you" (Gen. 12:1), was it a command or an invitation?

It was both. God's words to Abraham were a clear command, not an option. But it was a command that quickly flowed into a glorious promise. When you think about it, many of God's commands are invitations.

Jesus commanded a little twelve-year-old girl to rise from the dead. Taking her by the hand He said to her, "Get up, little girl!" (Luke 8:54, TLB). He directed her heart to beat, her lungs to swell, her eyes to open. He commanded her to begin consuming oxygen again. But His directive was also an invitation—a summons to life in a new dimension.

Imagine a door into a room that has Entrance over the door on one side, and Exit over the door on the other side. God often commands His children to step through a door that says You Obey Me on one side and I Bless You on the other.

If we obey Him in faith, putting our full trust in His will for our lives, we will one day find that He has called us into a higher, brighter, infinitely-more-fulfilling way of life. It was the same with Abraham. As this pagan man from the land of Ur heeded God's summons and walked into mystery, he was being invited into an incomparable destiny, beyond anything he could have conceived in his thoughts or dreams.

Although Abraham may not have consciously analyzed it, he might have received a big clue about how all these things would work out if he had simply counted the number of times God said, "I will" in that promise. In fact, God said it three times. (See Genesis 12:2.) In contrast, how many "you wills" are in there?

One.

Might this suggest to us that God's part is the doing part? "I will…I will…I will." That's all God. "You will" in this passage is not about doing; it's about being. "You will be a blessing." It's what God does that makes us who we are. The problems come in our lives when we take our "I will" and put it in place of His "I will."

The Bible tells us about a time when a mighty angel of great beauty did that very thing. His name was, Lucifer, son of the morning. A startling passage in the book of Isaiah laments his great fall:

> How you have fallen from heaven, O morning star, son of the dawn! You have been cast down to the earth, you who once laid low the nations! You said in your heart, "I will ascend to heaven; I will raise my throne above the stars of God; I will sit enthroned on the mount of assembly, on the utmost heights of the sacred mountain. I will ascend above the tops of the clouds; I will make myself like the Most High."
> —ISAIAH 14:12–14

How many "I wills" pop up in Lucifer's statement? Four. But putting his "I will" before God's "I will" has been nothing but disaster for him. Lucifer became Satan, the devil, and that same passage in Isaiah goes on to say: "But you are brought down to the grave, to the depths of the pit" (v. 15).

Juxtaposed against this self-will of Satan, we witness the words the Lord Jesus prayed on a dark night of agony in a garden called Gethsemane: "Father, if you are willing, please take this cup of suffering away from me. Yet I want your will to be done, not mine" (Luke 22:42).

Satan's favorite song is, "Me-me-me-me-me," and we've all sung along in that refrain. Feeling "in control" and taking life into our own hands is a strong narcotic.

In 1969, Frank Sinatra had a hit tune that became the signature song of his career. The lyrics record the proud, defiant words of a man near death who shakes his fist at heaven, and basically says, "Well, my life hasn't been perfect, but at least I've lived it for myself. I looked after Number One above all else, and now, at the end—even facing death and hell—I can sing, 'I did it my way'!"

It's interesting how popular this anthem to selfishness has been through the years. But the theme is as old as the Garden of Eden. The poet William Ernest Henley expressed much the same sentiments over one hundred years before Sinatra ever put his face in front of a microphone.

> It matters not how strait the gate
> How charged with punishments the scroll,
> I am the master of my fate:
> I am the captain of my soul.[1]

Whether we want to admit it or not, that's us. That's the spirit of mankind apart from acknowledging Jesus as Lord. Proud, independent, defiant, and self-reliant. Little gods ruling over our little worlds, bowing to no one, yielding to no one, serving ourselves and our own pleasure and convenience beyond all else. It's exactly what the Father of Lies offered our ancestors in the misty morning of our world:

> "You won't die. God knows the moment you eat from that tree, you'll see what's really going on. You'll be just like God, knowing everything."
> —GENESIS 3:4–5, THE MESSAGE

In our flesh, in our earthly nature, we want to be in control and call the shots. We want to travel down the My-Way Highway. Even as believers, we don't like to wait for God's will, God's way, and God's timing. And great as Abraham and Sarah may be in Scripture, the Bible shows us that they, too, fell into this impatient, independent pattern of thinking. Here is how this godly couple made a grab for life on their own terms, and found it to be a death grip.

THE BOOMERANG EFFECT

Listen, we can be hard on Abraham for going along with Sarah's scheme to shortcut God's plan and bring a child into the world through Hagar, but think about waiting ten years for an answer to your most fervent heart cry. How long do those years seem when we know God has told us something, but nothing happens for a decade? It's a long, long time.

We can all identify with getting impatient and trying to push the envelope now and then. And when we do that, when we first muscle our own will ahead of the Lord's and "take charge" of a frustrating situation, it feels pretty good. It feels like we're finally getting off the dime, finally making headway. And we can even reason with ourselves a bit, and say, "Well, this is probably what the Lord wanted anyway. Doesn't 'the Lord help those who help themselves'?"

That may have been how it seemed to Abraham and Sarah, at first. The Bible says, "So Abram had sexual relations with Hagar, and she became pregnant" (Gen. 16:4, NLT). Wow, just like that! After all those years of fruitless waiting, here was instant conception.

But exercising our own will, however satisfying it may seem initially, always has a boomerang effect. When you throw it out there in front of you, it has a way of circling back and smacking you between the eyes.

> When Hagar knew she was pregnant, she began to treat her mistress Sarai with contempt. Then Sarai said to Abram, "This is all your fault!...Now this servant of mine is pregnant, and she despises me, though I myself gave her the privilege of sleeping with you. The Lord will make you pay for doing this to me!"
> —GENESIS 16:4–5, NLT, AUTHOR'S PARAPHRASE

Trouble. Oh, such trouble. The boomerang swung around and came back as a curse. Abraham's once tranquil household became a battle zone between two bitterly unhappy women— the very atmosphere within the confines of those tents thick with tension and strife. The same thing can happen to any of us. When

God's promise of better life, Life², seems to be slip-sliding away from us, we may try to play God and force things to our own advantage, thinking "I'll get this done myself. God's not coming through, and I'll just have to take care of this."

We certainly have the freedom to do that, and we might have the skill to be successful at it. But let's not kid ourselves; the boomerang always comes back. It might take weeks or it might take years, but it will circle around in an unfailing arc to wound us and all that we treasure and love.

When the struggles between Hagar and Sarah finally boiled over, Hagar ran away, nearly perishing alone in the desert. God, however, sustained her in the wilderness and led her back to the family to have the baby.

> So Hagar gave Abram a son, and Abram named him Ishmael. Abram was eighty-six years old at that time.
> —GENESIS 16:15–16, NLT

Ishmael means "God hears with intelligence." Did that mean God hears in accordance with my intelligence? I'm reminded of those times when I pray, "Oh, God, this is what I need. Please, God, do my agenda. I've worked it all out and it's a reasonable thing to ask!"

That was the situation with Ishmael. He was a product of, "God, please bless my agenda." Rather than saying, "God, I want to do what You are blessing," it was saying, "God, I want You to bless what I am doing."

And what was the result? Well, the results have rolled on and on through the centuries and millennia. In verse 12, we read a prophecy about Ishmael:

He will be a wild donkey of a man; his hand will be against everyone and everyone's hand against him, and he will live in hostility toward all his brothers.

Doesn't that sound like the Middle East today? And the truth is, Ishmael became the father of the Arab race—the very ones living in such bitter hostility with the nation of Israel today.

"He will be a wild donkey of a man." It reminds me of what my grandma once called me. She said, "Kenny, you're a little jackass." (I still haven't recovered!)

Living on his own terms, trying to run ahead of God and "make life happen," Abraham produced an Ishmael. And so it is with you and me. If I push my own agenda over the Lord's plan for my life, I may make a mint, but eventually I'll make a mess. I may become rich and famous, but I will also bring trouble into my own home, and great heartache with it.

To me, one of the most dramatic scriptures comparing "life on our own terms" with Life², is in Paul's counsel to Timothy, his young friend in ministry:

People who want to get rich fall into temptation and a trap and into many foolish and harmful desires that plunge men into ruin and destruction. For the love of money is a root of all kinds of evil. Some people, eager for money, have wandered from the faith and pierced themselves with many griefs.
—1 TIMOTHY 6:9–10

Can't you just feel the pain—the bone-deep ache of grief and regret—throbbing in these words? Harmful desires…ruin and destruction…pierced with many griefs. The Greek term for "pierced" in verse 10 literally means to penetrate entirely, to transfix. We're not talking about a few psychological bruises and scrapes here; we're talking about a sword thrust of sorrow that pins you to the wall.

In startling contrast, those who place their lives and their resources in the Lord's hands, trusting in Him and looking to Him for everything, "take hold of the life that is truly life" (6:19).

Which is yet another way of saying, you will walk in Life².

THE STORY BEHIND THE STORY

As so frequently happens in Scripture, we have a story, and then a greater story behind it. So it is with Abraham's family and the conflict between Hagar and Sarah, Ishmael and Isaac.

> The child grew and was weaned, and on the day Isaac was weaned Abram held a great feast. But Sarah saw that the son whom Hagar the Egyptian had borne to Abraham was mocking, and she said to Abraham, "Get rid of that slave woman and her son, for that slave woman's son will never share in the inheritance with my son Isaac."
>
> The matter distressed Abram greatly because it concerned his son. But God said to him, "Do not be so distressed about the boy and your maidservant. Listen to whatever Sarah tells you, because it is through Isaac that your offspring will be reckoned. I will make the son of the maidservant into a nation also, because he is your offspring."
>
> Early the next morning Abraham took some food and a skin of water and gave them to Hagar. He set them on her shoulders and then sent her off with the boy. She went on her way and wandered in the desert of Beersheba.
>
> —GENESIS 21:8–14

Have you ever looked at one of those weird posters that depicts scenes on two different levels? You're looking at some typical two-dimensional depiction of something and then something clicks in your brain, your focus shifts, and a three dimensional scene suddenly jumps out at you.

My friend was telling me about one that showed the bottom of the sea. And then suddenly there was a shark swimming right out of the poster at him. Some people stare and stare at those posters, and can't get their eyes to make the switch. For others, the underlying 3-D picture jumps out immediately.

That's the way it is with the Ishmael-Isaac story. It's an absorbing true account of a family in ancient times—only eleven generations from Adam and Eve. But there is a deeper story behind the story, with a direct application to each one of us. Thankfully, we don't have to stare at it until our eyes cross and the underlying scene jumps out at us; the book of Galatians takes care of that!

> Abraham, remember, had two sons: one by the slave woman and one by the free woman. The son of the slave woman was born by human connivance; the son of the free woman was born by God's promise. This illustrates the very thing we are dealing with now. The two births represent two ways of being in relationship with God.
> —GALATIANS 4:22, THE MESSAGE

It's an amazing study, and one well worth your time. But for our purposes right now, let's cut to the chase. Ishmael represents salvation by works—trying to earn all the Brownie points you can on Earth so that you might be accepted in heaven. Isaac, however—the miracle child, the child of promise—represents salvation by faith: trusting in Christ and His sacrifice alone to make us right with God.

Jesus said, "If you believe in Me, I'll give you life" (John 6:40, author's paraphrase). It's done! On the cross, Jesus cried out, "*Tetélestai!*" "It is finished" (John 19:30). Paid in full. Transaction complete. Account closed.

You can study it out in Scripture, but this is what it comes down to: Ishmael is legalistic religion; Isaac is a loving relationship with God through Jesus Christ. Ishmael is life on my terms; Isaac is life on God's terms. Ishmael is what I'd rather hold onto; Isaac is what I get if I let go.

LETTING GO OF ISHMAEL

Here's the bottom line. If we want what God has for us, we have to let go of something. If we want life on His terms, we have to let go of life on our terms. And letting go isn't easy. Ask Abraham! He was deeply distressed at the thought of letting Ishmael go and sending him away—which may be a weak way to say it. The Hebrew word translated "distressed" literally means to "spoil by breaking into pieces." In other words, it was a shattering experience for the old man—as it may be for you and me when God asks us to let go of something we've been clinging to for a long, long time.

What kinds of things might He ask us to let go of, so that we might receive from Him?

Sometimes it's position. God may ask us to step down from some position or responsibility, just to serve Him without fanfare and behind the scenes for a season. But over time we've let some of our self-worth become wrapped around that title, and it's very hard to disengage ourselves.

Sometimes it's possessions. You don't need things to enjoy life; you need life to enjoy things! Jesus said, "Steep your life in God-reality, God-initiative, God-provisions. Don't worry about missing out. You'll find all your everyday human concerns will be met. Give your entire attention to what God is doing right now" (Matt. 6:32–34, THE MESSAGE).

Sometimes it's people. It might be an actual person that we need to let go of. Perhaps a son or daughter who needs some independence and some space—or the freedom to fail and learn from that failure. Maybe we need to let go of a friendship that we know very well is dragging us down and harming our relationship with Christ.

Sometimes it's location. We say, "Oh, I could never live there." Really? Not even if God asked you to? Or maybe we tell people, "I could never leave this part of the country. I've lived here all my life." Be careful. If we say "never" to the Lord, then He really isn't our Lord at all.

Sometimes it's expectations. We've imagined a scenario in our minds for months or even years. We've had it all planned, and could just imagine how it would all work out. But what if it doesn't? What if God's will leads in a different direction? Can we let our expectations go, for His sake?

Sometimes it's letting go of habits.

Sometimes it's letting go of our tithe—the first ten percent of our income that belongs to the Lord. In reality, of course, it all belongs to Him—and giving the tithe of our gross income simply acknowledges that reality. Some of the people in our church have taken that faith step this past year—people who had no idea how they could meet their obligations with ten percent less income. You should see some of the e-mails I've been getting. Couples and families have been telling me about provision and extra money "coming out of nowhere!"

Sometimes it's our priorities. It might mean letting go of some long-cherished plans.

Sometimes it's something good, not bad. How true it is that the good can become the enemy of the best. The last thing refined from gold is silver! Sometimes God may want us to release something worthy and good in our lives in order to give us something better.

All in all, the hardest thing for us to let go of is our desire to be in control. If we name Him as our Lord, we need to let go of that—even if it means prying our hands off that steering wheel one finger at a time.

I remember when I left a thriving business to enter the ministry.* I was twenty-nine years old, and involved in five part-nerships and three corporations, all of which were growing and yielding some sweet profits.

I recall sitting in a church service in the Chapel of the Cascades one day when God ordered an instant replay: He showed me a

---

* I must hasten to add here that I don't believe an ordained pastor is one bit higher on the commitment scale than an ordained plumber. Salt is spread over everything, and Christians need to be spread throughout the culture. God puts people where He wants.

picture of myself as a seven year old, responding to an evangelist's invitation, and going to the altar at the front of the church.

At the altar I promised God I would be a pastor one day. Later that day, I told my parents about my promise. They never mentioned it to me again, and I completely forgot about it.

And there I was, a motivated, happy businessman, set to become a millionaire by mid-thirties, and God spoiled it all by playing my promise back as clear as a movie in my mind.

And then He said, "I'm here to collect."

Deep down, I had no doubt that it was what God wanted. But how difficult it was to walk away from that business success! The enemy kept saying to me, "You'd better hold onto this. If you let go, God will never replace this opportunity."

I'm convinced that some people refuse to embrace Life^2 because it just seems so reckless. We feel so secure with our tight grip on everything familiar that we're reluctant to let go, afraid of receiving from the Lord with open and empty hands. But God requires an exchange. You can't take in an armload of life from heaven if you've already got an armload of earthly possessions and preoccupations.

The road forks, one highway climbing into the hill country of Life^2, and the other going straight on across the flat plain toward the horizon—the same old road taking you to the same old places.

A friend wrote me these words a couple of months ago: "The most significant moments in your days on earth may very be those frightening crossroads where the living God calls you to release something familiar and secure in order to receive something utterly unknown and mysterious. Your life hinges on these choices."

WILDLIFE

> Listen carefully: Unless a grain of wheat is buried in the
> ground, dead to the world, it is never any more than a grain
> of wheat. But if it is buried, it sprouts and reproduces itself
> many times over. In the same way, anyone who holds on to
> life just as it is destroys that life. But if you let it go, reckless
> in your love, you'll have it forever, real and eternal.
> —JOHN 12:24, THE MESSAGE

I had a friend in North Carolina tell me last week about how
he went to Texas and shot a nice buck on a 500-acre fenced-in
farm. I acted interested, but the idea of shooting animals in a
zoo doesn't really rev my engine. I don't even get jazzed about
shooting deer and elk with a high-powered rifle. When I hunt, I
go to Colorado and lead a pack horse nine miles into the wilderness, live off jerky, cheese, crackers, and hot chocolate for a week,
and try to get within twenty yards of an elusive bull elk so I can
stick him with an arrow. That's life in the wild, that's wildlife!

Remember that duckling I killed? It was wired by the Creator
to be reckless, wild, out of control. It wasn't meant to be boxed in
and manhandled (or even boy-handled). When I took control of
the duck, it lost its "wild" and then its life.

Your life is like that little duck. If you think you own it, you
kill it.

Life^2 happens only when you resist the temptation to control
your own life. Life^2 requires you to get reckless and let go of your
life. If you open your hands and drop the seed in the ground, if you
let the duckling go, if, reckless in your love, you let Jesus be not
only resident but president, He raises your life to a new power.

It takes reckless love. Many people think believing in Christ is simply a matter of mental assent: "Yes, I believe that. I believe Jesus Christ walked this earth. I believe He died and rose again for me." When you come to Christ on your terms, He's in your head. When you come to Christ on His terms, He's in your heart.

I'm no judge as to whether this "head knowledge" brings a person to salvation or not. That's between that man or woman and the Lord. But everything I understand about crossing from death to life tells me there's an element of risk involved.

It's Matthew getting up from his tax collection table and leaving it all behind to follow Jesus.

It's Saul of Tarsus turning his back on all his peers and all his training to serve the Name he had tried to annihilate.

It's Cornelius the Roman Centurion who risked his military career to hold an evangelistic meeting in his home.

Do you remember receiving Christ and feeling a little bit unnerved by what might be expected of you? I had ridiculous pictures in my mind of tap dancing on café tables, saying "Jesus loves you!" I didn't know what weird stuff was ahead for me. What if He asked me to spend my life in Africa living in some hut and eating grubs? It seemed like a risky business to follow the Lord, and I didn't really know what it would mean. Even so, I took a deep breath and made that step of faith: I let go of my old life and my old ways to follow Him.

Notice those two key words in the last sentence.

Let go.

I had to let go to receive eternal life, and I have to keep letting go to keep receiving the higher life. I wonder how many times the Holy Spirit has said those two words to me since I became a Christ-follower thirty-eight years ago. Times beyond number!

I am amazed at how much we as Christians hold onto life when life was given to us to lose.

Receiving Christ takes reckless love, and remaining in Christ does as well. Why? Because He has told us that life in Him will sometimes involve pruning. In the book of John, He declared: "I am the true grapevine, and my Father is the gardener. He cuts off every branch of mine that doesn't produce fruit, and he prunes the branches that do bear fruit so they will produce even more" (John 15:1–2, NLT).

I remember pruning the willow tree in our back yard some years ago. We had a little above-ground pool for the kids to swim in, and twigs and leaves from our overgrown willow kept falling into the water. So Linda told me to go out there and prune it.

Ah, but when you put a chainsaw into a guy's hands, you never know what the result will be! I pruned it all right, but I realized after awhile that I was trying to be too artistic about it. You know, you cut a branch off on the left and then you have to cut another branch on the right to balance it out. By the time I had finished balancing everything out, there wasn't much there but the trunk.

It looked awful. In spite of myself, I kept thinking about one of those lurid Asherah poles in the Old Testament. Linda almost screamed when she saw my handiwork. "You've killed it! It will never grow back!" Yet within a year, it had grown more large and full than it was before I took the saw to it. I couldn't believe how much it grew.

Sometimes God might ask you to let go of something that almost seems to be a part of you. He prunes something out of your life, and you say, "Oh, I can't believe You'd take that from me." And then a year later you look at your life and say, "Whoa, look at all He has given me! What I had was good—but it was nothing compared to this!"

Jesus said, "I've come that you might have more and better life" (John 10:10, THE MESSAGE). That's a happy prospect, but it's a little unnerving to allow Him to take the chain saw to different limbs, precious parts of your life. It takes faith. That's crazy love. Reckless love.

When God played that video of me as a seven year old promising to be a pastor, I remember the perplexity I felt. I loved being in business. Was He going to take that from me? I loved swimming with sharks. I loved being creative and figuring out a way to turn setbacks into stepping stones, turn crises into cash cows. I had to decide whether Jesus Christ was going to strip me or bless me, love me or use me, rip me off or lift me up, diminish my life or expand it.

Just recently in my devotions I read about the community of people in the region called the Gerasenes, on the eastern shore of the Sea of Galilee. Jesus did a stunning miracle in that place, healing a demon-possessed man who had terrorized the community for a long time. In the grip of a legion of demons (a Roman legion in that time had six to seven thousand soldiers) and so powerful he couldn't be bound with ropes or chains, this man embodied great darkness and evil within their midst.

But the demons were like little toy soldiers in the presence of God's mighty Son. Pleading with Him not to banish them, the evil spirits begged to be sent into a large herd of pigs contentedly grazing on the hillside. Jesus complied with the request, and the herd went wild, plunging over a cliff into the sea.

When the people heard about the pigs and saw the Wild Man of the Gerasenes clothed and sitting calmly at the Lord's feet, they begged Him to leave their area. For those brief hours, they had the Creator of the universe visiting their shores. They had One who might have walked among them and healed their sick and taught the way to eternal life.

But He had messed with their pigs, and they asked him to leave. He had healed a crazy man, and it scared them. Too much change, too fast. They would rather hold onto life the way they had always known it, rather than risk the unknown wonders and perils of Life².

On the one hand, they had the Savior. On the other hand, He had messed with their stuff and pruned their profit. (Indeed, the most sensitive nerve in the body is the one that runs from our heart to our wallet.) They could have hugged Jesus, but they were too busy hugging their purses. God can't pour His riches into hands that are already full.

In a good gospel movie, the choir would break into the chorus of "Let Go and Let God" at this point, but this wasn't a movie, this was real life. This "Bay of Pigs" thing was as shocking to them as it was to me when God said twenty-seven years ago, "I'm here to collect." If I were sitting in front of you right now, I could look you straight in the face and say with all honesty that I'm so glad I didn't ask Jesus to just get in His boat and go, leaving me alone. I decided right there to waste my life on God, believing that I would have the rest of this life and all of eternity to recover.

I've learned over and over that when I turn a new part of my life over to the control of Lord Jesus, at first it feels to me like things are out of control. Pigs start running off cliffs. Things get crazy. I want to make a declaration of independence and cut myself free from His control.

I remember flying a kite at D-Lake on the Oregon coast when I was a kid. It's the kite-flying center of Oregon, and it was a windy day, so there were dozens of colorful kites in the air. But then the wind gusted so strong that my kite string broke. I expected my kite to soar higher in the sky and just vanish from sight. But it didn't. It started flipping and flopping, and it dove into the sand, crunching the frame.

I guess people are like that. The person who claims to be utterly free, not obligated to God or to anybody else, usually lives a tragic life that ends with a crash. On the other hand, the happiest, highest flying, most creative people on earth are those who live connected to the God of Life[2] by a strong line of faith, allowing God to direct and control their lives.

How much does He want from you? Everything! He wants your pigs, your possessions, your position, and your passion. Yes, He wants your heart. The most difficult thing to let go is self. It's all you have and all you are for all He has and all He is. He doesn't want shares of your life, He wants controlling interest. He doesn't want a little piece of your heart, He wants the whole enchilada.

When we follow Jesus Christ with all our hearts, He'll upset a few of our apple carts along the way. He will scramble our plans. He will walk us through realms of mystery and perplexity. He will stretch us farther than we thought we could ever stretch. As Mrs. Beaver told Lucy in the opening volume of the *Chronicles of Narnia*, "He isn't a tame lion...but He's good."[2]

But how tedious life would be without risk. God built that desire for adventure into every one of us. That's why movies like *The Lord of the Rings* make so much money: Little Frodo left his beloved Shire to brave perils and terrors, risking his life to save

Middle Earth. There's something in all of us that says, "That's the story! That's what it's all about!"

It's an adventure, but it's scary because we're not sure what will be "added" to our "venture." That's the way it is when we follow Jesus Christ with all our hearts. He'll upset a few of our apple carts along the way. He will scramble our plans. He will walk us through realms of mystery and perplexity. He will stretch us farther than we thought we could ever stretch.

Jesus said, "Anyone who holds on to life just as it is destroys that life. But if you let it go, reckless in your love, you'll have it forever, real and eternal" (John 12:25, THE MESSAGE). If we hold on to our world as it is, it becomes a death grip. If we put all our chips on Ishmael, the child of our self-effort, we'll never have an Isaac, the child of miracle and promise. If we cling to life on our own terms, we'll kill it. God loved you with a reckless love, and He's asking you to reciprocate.

You'll never tap into God's riches unless you take a risk.

CHAPTER 5

LIFE WITH A VIEW

God sees more—so much more—in you than you see in you.

I should have been preparing for a meeting, but just for fun, I started squaring numbers on my pocket calculator. It's not one of those elaborate mini-super-computers in a smooth leather sheath that well-armed Calculus students wear into class these days. It's just your cheap, basic model for figuring out things I should probably be able to do in my head.

So I started with two times two, and just went on from there. Here's just a little progression.

$2^2 = 4,$
$4^2 = 16,$
$16^2 = 256,$
$256^2 = 65,536,$
$65,536^2 = 4,294,967,296.$

I stopped there, surprised at how rapidly those numbers shoot into the stratosphere. Well, actually I stopped because my calculator went into lockdown—apparently in jeopardy of blowing its little chip. Why? Because when you square something mathematically, when you times something by itself, the results rocket right off the chart.

What then, is Life^2?

That's the metaphor I've been using in this book to describe a level of life for believers that's far-and-away beyond what most of us conceive or expect. It is life times life—who you are times who you are. It is who the living God made you to be, right now, on this side of heaven.

But this is something more than a metaphor for me. We're talking about an all-knowing, all-powerful, infinite God, who has said to us in His Son, "The thief's purpose is to steal and kill and destroy. My purpose is to give life in all its fullness" (John 10:10, TLB).

I know what my definition of fullness might be, but what is God's definition? Does it quickly blast my calculator's capacity? Do its exponential implications soar beyond imagination? Sometimes in the course of our years of walking with God, He unexpectedly opens our eyes, giving us a glimpse of life on a level so much higher than the way we have conceived it and lived it.

It's like being a child and seeing your first butterfly. Or being startled by a brilliant rainbow in a moment's gap between storms. Or catching a glimpse of castle turrets in the towering golden clouds a minute before sunset. Or stepping out your front door before dawn on a winter morning to see the morning star, low on the horizon, burning with silver fire.

Moments like those can take your breath away.

No, we can't live at that level all of the time, or even most of the time. Not while we possess flesh-and-blood bodies and walk about on a broken planet. After all, Peter didn't walk on water every time he crossed the Sea of Galilee. The three disciples didn't spend a year on top of the Mount of Transfiguration. Paul wasn't caught up into the third heaven every few days.

These were glimpses—profound, life-transforming, faith-stretching glances behind the curtain of visibility.

Abraham had several such look-sees into the realm of Life[2]. And there came a time in this man's life when God sent his calculator beyond capacity. As it happened, he was 99 years old when he experienced this particular close encounter with the Lord:

> The Lord appeared to him and said, "I am God Almighty; walk before me and be blameless. I will confirm my covenant between me and you and will greatly increase your numbers."
>
> —GENESIS 17:1–2

At this time, remember, Abraham and Sarah were still without a child of their own. So when God said to Abraham, "I will...greatly increase your numbers" (even though He had told him already), He was talking about something that was still beyond the patriarch's comprehension.

What was Abraham's response? Verse 3 says that he "fell face-down." Facedown isn't a position we normally aspire to in life. It brings back memories of junior high and falling on the track in the 880, or doing a face plant on the ski slope.

When I see that term "face down," I can't help but think of my first experience with a tree stand. We were archery hunting in our favorite hunting place in the rugged mountains on the edge of Hell's Canyon in Oregon.

On this particular hunt, I found a great water hole the elk loved to drink from and wallow in. The mountain oasis was in the middle of a meadow, with three large pine trees standing like soldiers at the water's edge.

I called the meadow "Magic Meadow." I could never seem to get near the elk that drank there, because the trunks of the few trees around the water hole didn't provide enough cover.

So my friend Lonny, a carpenter, made me a plywood tree stand. It was solid, but very heavy. Lonny added two shoulder straps so I could carry the thirty pound stand on my back all the way in to Magic Meadow. He offered to go with me and help me secure the stand.

When we got to the water hole late that evening, Lonny watched from the ground as I climbed one of the trees with the stand on my back. When I reached a height of about twenty five feet, the branch I was standing on broke.

When I fell, the tree stand somehow came off my back. I did a face-first into the ground; one corner of the heavy stand gouged the earth about four inches from my face, and then the stand crashed into my head. It knocked me out for a few seconds, and when I came to I was seeing stars. I felt something warm and wet on my face. "Oh no," I thought, "I'm bleeding bad!" My vision hadn't focused yet, and Lonny was just a blur as he ran over to me. When things started to come into focus, I looked at Lonny, expecting to see a look of alarm on his face.

To my surprise, he was smiling! What in the world?

"Are you really hurt," he asked, "or do you just feel crappy?" Long story short, I had fallen into a gooey cow pie, face first. Once I recovered a little, we had a good belly laugh. We decided I should just leave my face like it was until we got back to camp.

Just at dark, I came walking into camp and approached the other two guys in our party who were standing around a campfire. The forest roared with laughter as I acted out the story, complete with makeup. When they recount the story these days they say that when I smiled, my teeth looked like three marsh-mallows on top of a big chocolate cake.

That's the mental picture I have to deal with when someone says, "Face down." Face down is not something that appeals to me. I imagine most people feel somewhat the same way.

If, however, you find yourself in a private interview with the living God, that's really the only logical place to be. In the spir-itual realm, facedown gives you a better view of the landscape than standing on a ladder.

God had just reaffirmed a promise to Abraham that challenged the old man's grip on life-as-he-understood-it, and he fell before the Lord in worship. So it is with us. The more God blesses you, the more you fall in love with Him, the more you want to worship Him. *Father, You are so good—so good!*

It's about the Bless-er, more than the bless-ing.

As the passage continues, the Lord expands on this outpouring of grace.

WHAT'S IN A NAME?

"As for me, this is my covenant with you: You will be the father of many nations. No longer will you be called Abram; your name will be Abraham, for I have made you a father of many nations. I will make you very fruitful; I will make nations of you, and kings will come from you. I will establish my covenant as an everlasting covenant between me and you and your descendants after you for the generations to come, to be your God and the God of your descendants after you."

—GENESIS 17:4–7

Abram had been his name for nearly a century, and he probably assumed that's what it would be until his dying day. But God changed his name to Abr**AH**am. What is that added "AH"? What's that all about? Three things.

First, "AH" means upgraded

I'm highly computer illiterate and totally computer dependent. Thankfully, our tech guys at the church take good care of me. Several years ago they put a new "chip" (I think that's what they called it) in my computer. By faith I believed them when they said the new chip would greatly increase the capacity of my computer. Of course it would. After all, it had a whole bunch of giga-somethings!

By changing his name to Abraham, God is increasing Abram's capacity and drawing out his full potential. God says, "I hardwired you, Abraham. I know the capacity of your circuit board. You're loaded. There's more! Just believe me and I'll show you how to live deeper, higher, larger. Upgrade your thinking about Me, about yourself." "AH" means upgraded.

Second, "AH" means multiplied

How would you feel if God offered to double the quality and quantity of your life right now? Would you take Him up on it? He wants to do that, and more. Much more. "Life squared" is you times you, and even more than that, it's God in you. God wants strengthen you, multiply you, increase your life exponentially, explosively, abundantly. "AH" means multiplied.

Third, "AH" means reflected

The "AH" in Abraham is like a mirror. In Hebrew, inserting "AH" into a word means "to reveal the heart of." God wants

AbrAHam's life to reveal His own divine capacity, intensity, generosity, and magnanimity.

My name, Ken, in Hebrew means "priest." "Ken-AH" would mean "to reveal the heart of the priest." To me, that means that my life can actually reveal the heart of Jesus Christ, our High Priest.

By renaming Abram, God was actually promising to bring out of him more than he had ever imagined. Abram means "father of many; father of honor." Abraham means more, much more; it means "father of nations; father who brings honor to God"!

God saw more in Abram than Abram saw in Abram. He sees more in me than I've seen yet. He sees more in you than you do.

God had a plan to make Abraham prolific, mega-productive, and mega-reproductive. God says, "I want to go beyond your heart's desire to father a child with Sarah. I want to make you the father of nations—revealing the hugeness of My heart when this happens in your life and in the lives of those who follow after you."

This was my passion for writing this book. More than that, it's been the heart of my ministry over the last twenty-five years: To declare that God sees more in you than you do. He sees more in you than anyone has ever seen in you. As I am writing this line, I am thinking of you reading this book. I am praying for you. I am praying the "AH" light will come on for you. I'm asking God to give you what I call an AH-HA moment. I want you to catch a glimpse of the hugeness of His promises and His plans for you. He wants His life to be so strong in you that people actually believe there is an AH-God because of the AH in your life.

Think back in your earliest memory to every evaluation of your worth, competence, or potential. Perhaps someone affirmed you along the way, and you will always remember their words. Maybe it was your dad or mom, a pastor, a teacher, a coach, or a friend. Those words that you received, that assessment of who you were and what you could become has stayed with you all these years, and you have drawn hope and strength from it.

Or maybe the valuations that come to your mind are dark and hurtful ones. You remember someone—maybe an important someone—who pretty much wrote you off. Someone who should have loved and treasured you ignored you or treated you like trash. In so many words, that individual told you that you were unimportant or awkward or dumb or ugly, and that you would never amount to much in life. And those words have weighed you down through the years like a hundred pound backpack, bending you over, eroding your confidence, and leeching away your joy. Because of what significant people in your life have said, you may not have a very high opinion of you.

But He does.

He says, "I know the plans I have for you...plans to prosper you and not to harm you, plans to give you hope and a future" (Jer. 29:11). He sees what you are right now, and what you can be, as you step out on faith and believe Him.

BEGINNING WITH THE INVISIBLE

People tend to think of a "blessed life" in terms of having and doing. What's a blessed life in America? According to popular consensus, it's having more and doing more. But we all know people who have a lot and do a lot, and are a long way from what we would call "blessed." It's also about being more.

In Genesis 17:4, God uses the words, "You will be...." That's future.

In verse 5, He says, "You will no longer be...." That's past.

Again in verse 5, He says, "Your name will be...." And that's me! That's who I am. God says, "I'm going to change you, I'm going to elevate your life."

How do we find this elevated life? Through faith in God's Word, and what He clearly says about each one of us. Maybe you don't see much promise in yourself right now. No matter. Remember that God is the one who speaks of things that are not as though they were. Because in His sight, they are before they are!

In the account we've been considering in Genesis 17, there's an interesting switch in tense between verses 4 and 5. In verse 4, God tells Abraham, "I will make you a father of many nations," and then—almost in the same breath in verse 5—He says, "I have made you a father of many nations."

Which is it? Is it past tense or future tense? Is it that God will, or that He already has?

Both.

As time-bound creatures, relating to an eternal God can leave us perplexed. Jesus once stunned a group of religious leaders by saying, "Before Abraham was, I Am!" (John 8:58). When Moses fell before the burning bush in the Midian wilderness, he asked God, "Whom shall I say sent me?" And God replied, "Tell them I Am sent you." (See Exodus 13:14.)

That's God. He is. He has always been, He lives in this moment, and He always will be. Most everything you and I call "reality" right now is encased in a tiny, fragile, space-time bubble. But God infinitely transcends that bubble—He is the eternal I Am, past, present, and future. In the book of Revelation, Jesus declared: "I am the Alpha and the Omega [the A and Z]...who is, and who was, and who is to come, the Almighty" (Rev. 1:8).

God often speaks of things as already done before they are done, because He knows that we are going to believe what He says and they are going to get done in the visible realm.

Everything visible begins in the invisible realm. Walk into an electronics store or down the hardware aisle at Wal-Mart, and pick up half a dozen different items. Each one of those objects or contraptions started in somebody's mind. Somebody had an idea for something that did not yet exist, but would exist. Before the first vegetable peeler ever came to be, there was a vegetable peeler in someone's mind. He or she woke up in the night and said, "Why of course! How simple. I've got to write that idea down." And soon that idea took form in time and space. The idea became reality.

God gave that creativity, whether the inventor realized it or not; and what was visible only in their mind became a physical, touchable, useable product in almost every kitchen drawer in America.

But what if God has an idea? What then? What if He has an idea about you—about your potential in Christ? Our eternal God decides something, declares it in Scripture, and offers you the opportunity to bring that invisible something into the visible world by your faith.

You and I have the potential to believe impossibilities into possibilities, by faith. Remember the story of the two blind men who followed behind Jesus, crying out to Him for mercy? They finally caught up to Him inside a house, and Jesus spoke to them:

> He asked them, "Do you believe that I am able to do this?" "Yes, Lord," they replied. Then he touched their eyes and said, "According to your faith will it be done to you"; and their sight was restored.
>
> —MATTHEW 9:28–30

The Message renders Jesus' last comment, "Become what you believe" (v. 29, THE MESSAGE). God wired us to walk and function by faith through all our days. God sees who I could be, then gives me His Word as a basis for becoming that person. The Bible says:

> You saw me before I was born. Every day of my life was recorded in your book. Every moment was laid out before a single day had passed.
>
> —PSALM 139:16, NLT

Perhaps you are reading these words thinking to yourself, "If my life is a book, then it's pretty messed up. I've written my own story, and it's not a good read. Nothing seems to be turning out for me." That's the wonderful thing about receiving Jesus and being born again. God will start a new book with you. Today begins a crisp, clean, white page, and He will make sure that your best chapters are still ahead of you. God sees who He made you to be; He speaks it, and when you believe it, you become who He made you to be.

You think it's too late for you? That's a lie from the Evil One. It's never too late while you draw breath. That's the whole point of this episode in Abraham's life. The man who was sure it was too late for a miracle stepped right into one. And it changed everything—right into the 21st Century.

A LAUGHING MATTER?

God also said to Abraham:

> "As for Sarai your wife, you are no longer to call her Sarai; her name will be Sarah. I will bless her and will surely give you a

son by her. I will bless her so that she will be the mother of nations; kings of peoples will come from her."

—Genesis 17:15–16

How do we respond when God gives us a glimpse of His desired future—a peek behind the curtain of who He sees us to be?

Abraham fell facedown again. Only this time he wasn't worshiping, he was laughing. He literally collapsed with laughter. The Bible even records his inmost thoughts in that moment:

Abraham fell facedown; he laughed and said to himself, "Will a son be born to a man a hundred years old? Will Sarah bear a child at the age of ninety?"

—Genesis 17:17–18

Oh yeah, sure. That's who we're going to be? Old and withered as we are? You bet!

Sarah had a good chuckle, too:

Sarah laughed within herself, "An old woman like me? Get pregnant? With this old man of a husband?"

—Genesis 18:12, The Message

We're going to have kids at this age? I'm going to wear maternity clothes and nurse a baby at age 90? Oh, that's a laugh!

You see, sometimes being who God says I am is, well, almost laughable! I look in the mirror and what do I see? Then I look in God's Word, and read what the Bible has to say about me; it just seems like such a wild mismatch. I can't call it absurd, because it's there in the Book. And I do "believe" it on at least one level, because I have staked my life and eternity on the utter veracity of His Word. But if I were to literally, totally believe what He says about me, well, we're talking about an experience that seems light-years out of my everyday reach. Consider just a few examples:

- ❧ I was chosen by God before the earth and the solar system existed (Eph. 1:4).

- ❧ I can do all things through Christ who strengthens me (Phil. 4:13).

- ❧ I am a friend of God (John 15:14–15).

- ❧ I possess, at this moment, immortality. I will literally live forever (John 3:15–16; John 10:28; Rom. 6:23).

- ❧ I am strengthened with all power (Col. 1:11).

- ❧ I am an ambassador of Jesus Christ (2 Cor. 5:20).

- ❧ I have the mind of Christ (1 Cor. 2:16).

- ❧ I have access to the full riches of complete understanding (Col. 2:2).

- ❧ I possess the very righteousness of God (2 Cor. 5:21).

- ❧ I am—right now—a citizen of heaven (Phil. 3:20).

- ❧ I have a share in the inheritance of God's only Son (Heb. 9:15; 1 Pet. 1:4).

- ❧ I have the mighty Spirit of the living God in residence within me (John 14:17; Rom. 8:9; 1 Cor. 3:16).

⇥ I have a relationship with Christ that moves the very angels with wonder (1 Pet. 1:12).

Yes, you might say, I've heard all that. Hear it again! And I challenge you to pick even one of those statements and seriously think through the implications. These aren't just nice religious words or Christian clichés, they are literal realities, as real as the chair in which you sit, as real as this morning's newspaper, whether we realize them or understand them or not. It's way over the top. It just seems like it can't be. It could make you fall on your face and laugh, as Abraham laughed.

When you look in the mirror of Gods' Word and see who God says you are, it is a staggering, mind-blowing portrait. The apostle John tried to express it, but seemed to run out of words:

> Yes, dear friends, we are already God's children, right now, and we can't even imagine what it is going to be like later on.
>
> —1 JOHN 3:2, TLB

You can see these truths about your real identity, your real potential on the page, but maybe you still have difficulty bringing those things into any real assessment of your actual future. Here's my counsel: Ask the Holy Spirit to give you a glimpse of what it really means to function in these truths. Catch sight of the sunlit mountain range on the near horizon through breaks in the fog. Wrap your hands of faith around any of those truths and grip it the way you would grip a rope after you've fallen partway down a cliff. The rope will hold. Because the One on the other end will never let go.

FAITH IS NOT SIGHT

In Genesis 15:6, the text simply says that Abraham believed God. Faith is following God before I know where. Faith is waiting for God without knowing when. Faith is expecting a miracle without knowing how. And faith is trusting in God's purpose and love without knowing why this is happening.

It's the difference between looking and seeing. A lot of people look; but you need to see in the invisible realm. Faith is not sight! Sight is just how life looks right now; faith is believing what God says life is going to look like.

Seeing like this takes time, because faith is tested over time. That's what this stay on earth is all about—strengthening your faith muscle in the gymnasium of daily living. Once you get to heaven, you won't need that kind of strengthening. Faith will have become sight! It is the progress you make here and now, in these few years on earth, that will make all the difference for you on the other side.

We read the highlights of Abraham's life in the Bible, but there were "low-lights," too. As we've seen, he tucked tail and ran to Egypt when a famine hit rather than believing what God had assured him about His provision and blessing. He had an attack of cowardice in Egypt, lied to the leaders of the land, and put his wife in danger to save his own skin. And then, when God didn't seem to be answering his prayer for a child fast enough, he went along with Sarah in an ill-fated scheme to answer their own prayers through a second wife.

But things began to change—when he was 99!

Sometimes you and I feel overwhelmed by our life circumstances, and our prayers begin to consist of, "Oh God, please change this situation. Please fix this problem. Please take away this heartache. Please deliver me from this trial." And because He loves us, He will sometimes do those things.

But God is more interested in changing me on the inside than changing things outside of me. He is more interested in adding muscle to my faith than He is pulling me out of every problem and challenge I have to face.

I can't take what I have into eternity, but I will take who I am into eternity. And when you think about it, it's a pretty short run here on this planet.

The more you find out about who God is, the more you find out about who you are. And when you focus on finding out who God wants you to be and begin searching His Word with discipline and diligence—with an open, believing heart—life begins to take on a new dimension.

Which is another way to say you've caught a glimpse of Life^2.

You Have It in You

> Now the Lord was gracious to Sarah as he had said, and the Lord did for Sarah what he had promised. Sarah became pregnant and bore a son to Abraham in his old age, at the very time God had promised him. Abraham gave the name Isaac to the son Sarah bore him.
>
> —GENESIS 21:1–3

Abraham and Sarah had a son in them—the fulfillment of their fondest dreams.

But they had such difficulty believing God's promise. When it came to bearing a miracle child, they didn't think they had it in them, and neither did anyone else.

And sometimes you think you don't have it in you. Well, if God says you do, you do. God sees more in me than anyone else sees in me; and what He sees comes forth. How does it happen? Faith in His Word. This struggling, cynical, sometimes-despairing world of our needs people who know and believe and feed on God's Word, and grow strong in spirit.

God named the little boy Isaac. Laughter. Isn't that interesting? Why would God give him a name like that? Because both Abraham and Sarah had laughed at the prospect of having a child. And now for the rest of their lives, whenever they saw their son, whenever they spoke his name, they would be reminded that God gets the last laugh.

The fact is, people may laugh about what God says about me, but if I believe Gods' Word, guess who gets the last laugh? God and I get the last laugh! It really doesn't matter what anyone else says about me or how anyone else evaluates me. If I believe what God says about me, I will become who God says I am.

I like the story about the two caterpillars crawling along across the dirt, looking up to see a majestic butterfly with great colored wings fluttering up above them.

"Whoa!" one said to the other. "You'll never get me up in one of those!"

This book is all about living at a higher level. God has more for you and doesn't want you to settle for a caterpillar life. And all this is based on faith in His Word. The writer of the book of Hebrews declares that "the fundamental fact of existence is that this trust in God, this faith, is the firm foundation under everything that makes life worth living. It's our handle on what we can't see" (Heb. 11:1).

The firm foundation under everything that makes life worth living. You and I need a faith foundation like this if we're going to build a life with a view. It's impossible to build a skyscraper on a chicken-coop foundation. Believing what God says about me, about my situation and about my potential, is a foundation for moving from life to Life².

Sometimes we're afraid to believe. We're afraid to go out on a limb, afraid to go higher, afraid to trust God for more. "I tried that once," you say, "and I fell flat on my face."

So what? Welcome to the human race. Abraham fell flat on his face several times, remember? But along the way he also made some great strides in his faith. And at the end of it all, he became one of two people in all the Old Testament whom God specifically called "friend."

God is in the people-changing business. He is certainly changing me—week by week changing who I am. I'm not the man I could be or should be, but neither am I the man that I was! This isn't theory. It isn't stained-glass religious platitude. It's real. It's actually happening. He is changing me from the inside out. Life is becoming better, larger, taller. Which simply means I am ever-so-slowly-but-steadily becoming more like Jesus.

AIR RIGHTS

I have preached a lot of messages in twenty-five years of ministry, but nothing means more to me than this: calling God's people to open up to all God has for them in life.

I think that's the heart of God. God saying, "I have more! Don't live a squalid, squatters' life. I've got more for you."

Five months ago I was in Chicago for a convention. We had a two-hour break between meetings, and my wife, Linda, talked me into going on an architectural tour via boat on the Chicago River. Quite honestly, it may not have been my first choice for spending our two hours. I'm not a student of architecture by any means, but Linda loves architecture and décor. So we climbed on board for a two-hour tour. (I got fifty "awesome husband" points just for getting on the boat!)

The tour guide was well versed in both the architectural history and the current building activity in the windy city. He showed us one huge skyscraper that was being built by the Trump Group, and mentioned that people would pay more than a million dollars for a small penthouse near the top. I began to count the stories, multiply by the number of windows per story, and then multiply that by a million bucks. My mental calculator crashed somewhere around two billion dollars.

The guide went on to say that many of these cash-cow skyscrapers were built on property permanently owned by someone other than the builders. He showed us the underground train tracks of the Union Railway and went on to explain that when Chicago land values skyrocketed in the 1920s, Union Railways tore up their tracks, dug tunnels for new tracks and sold "air rights" above their city acreage.

At that moment, I heard the voice of another Guide, invisible, but speaking clearly to my spirit. "I purchased air rights for you when I died on the cross and rose from the dead." I was stunned by what I heard in my heart. "Don't be a ground-hugging Christian, Ken," the Voice went on to say. "Don't live a single-story life; I have purchased a skyscraper life for you. Don't live a squatty little life; don't live a single-story life. You can live a skyscraper life!

You can have life with a view. You can see what I see about you. Open your eyes and see—believe Me."

In other words, my life can rise to new levels on the basis of my identification with the ultimate air rights, the resurrection life Jesus Christ purchased and pioneered for me.

Life is more than just what we have or what we do. It's also about who we are, who we can become. And when you start finding out who God says you are, and you start building on your relationship with God, everything in life changes.

Philippians 3:20 says, "We are citizens of heaven" (NLT). It doesn't say we will be; it says we are. This world desperately needs people who believe in the potential God put in them and who believe in what the Word of God says about them.

People just like you.

CHAPTER 6

FOUNTAIN OF YOUTH

You will never approach the Fountainhead of life with a
thirsty heart, and leave with less than you came.

Life had somehow skidded sideways, right into a dead-end.

A homeless, pregnant run-away, she had reached the
ragged end of her strength, collapsing on the hot sands
of the unforgiving desert. Then, just as she was about to give up
on everything, she heard a sound, perhaps the last sound she had
expected to hear.

Water.

It was the delicious, bubbling, trickling, musical sound of
flowing water. Was she dreaming? Water—in this desolate place?
Streams in the desert?

The Bible never really tells us whether Hagar had sought out the
spring of water in her thirst, or if the Lord had simply directed her
steps so that she found life at the point of her greatest need.

I'm betting on the second option!

WELL OF THE LIVING ONE

The book of Genesis simply tells us that the Angel of the Lord found her there, at a natural well in a dry and barren land. He found her, but He had never really lost her. Not for a minute. The Lord knew all there was to know about this Egyptian servant girl who had become a second wife to Abraham.

Even so, He asked her a question:

> "Hagar, servant of Sarai, where have you come from, and where are you going?" "I'm running away from my mistress Sarai," she answered.
> —GENESIS 16:7

The Angel of the Lord—whom many Bible scholars believe to a pre-New Testament appearance of Jesus, God's Son, in angelic form—knew that Hagar was not only worried about her own life, she was deeply concerned about the life of her unborn child. What would become of them? How could they survive? What would they do?

She found herself, as David would express it a thousand years later, in the valley of the shadow of death. But as with David, God was with her and had a plan for her, and her child, too:

> Then the angel of the Lord told her, "Go back to your mistress and submit to her." The angel added, "I will so increase your descendants that they will be too numerous to count."
> —GENESIS 16:9–10

That encounter by the little desert well filled the young woman with wonder. God had found her! God had cared enough to look for her and locate her in the wilderness. He loved her enough to gently ask about where she was in life, rather than harshly condemning her. And finally, He spoke to a mother-to-be's concern for her unborn child:

> The angel of the Lord also said to her: "You are now with child and you will have a son. You shall name him Ishmael, for the Lord has heard of your misery."
> —GENESIS 16:11

The word *misery* in the original language comes from a term that means "depressed in mind, or circumstances." Hagar had hit bottom, her mind gripped with darkness and despair. But the Lord saw her need, provided fresh water for her thirst, direction for her life, and a promise that rekindled her hope, giving her a reason to live again.

It was one of those amazing moments in life where God steps in, pulls us out of the swamp, renews His promises, and sets us on a fresh course.

As for Hagar, she never wanted to forget that moment when the Lord saw her need and spoke life to her:

> She gave this name to the Lord who spoke to her: "You are the God who sees me," for she said, "I have now seen the One who sees me." That is why the well was called Beer Lahai Roi [well of the Living One who sees me].
> —GENESIS 16:13–14

Hagar called God the Living One. She had been facing despair and death, and the Living One found her and directed her to the water that would save her. And Hagar learned that day that there was One who could rescue her, provide for her, direct her, and pour new life into her. God is Life, He is the well of eternal aliveness.

Five chapters later in Genesis, God did it again. Once again, years later, Hagar found herself forced away from Abraham's home, into the dry wilderness. And once again the Living One saw her distress:

> Then God opened her eyes and she saw a well of water. So she went and filled the skin with water and gave the boy a drink.
>
> —GENESIS 21:19

What a powerful sentence that is! God opened her eyes and she saw a well of water. That's what this book is all about, and that is my prayer for everyone who reads its pages. That God would open our eyes to see the well of Living Water so near at hand to each one of us. He comes to us when we're out of ideas, out of directions, out of options, out of money, and sometimes very nearly out of hope. He opens our eyes to the fountain so very near to us, and invites us to drink.

Leaving Hagar at the well in the desert, we can fast forward a couple thousand years to another well, another woman, and another encounter with the Living One.

LIVING WATER

Jesus and His disciples had entered the little Samaritan village of Sychar, and while He rested at the town well, His disciples went out in search of food. As He sat there, the Bible tells us that a woman, a Samaritan, came to draw water:

> Jesus said, "Would you give me a drink of water?"...The Samaritan woman, taken aback, asked, "How come you, a Jew, are asking me, a Samaritan woman, for a drink?" (Jews

in those days wouldn't be caught dead talking to Samaritans.)
Jesus answered, "If you knew the generosity of God and who
I am, you would be asking me for a drink, and I would give
you fresh, living water."

—JOHN 4:7–10, THE MESSAGE

Jesus did what no proper Jewish man in that day would have
ever done—started a conversation with the woman. It seems
familiar, doesn't it? A well, a thirsty woman, and God's Son with
an offer of life—fountains of never-ending life!

Jesus said, "Everyone who drinks this water will get thirsty
again and again. Anyone who drinks the water I give will
never thirst—not ever. The water I give will be an artesian
spring within, gushing fountains of endless life."

—JOHN 4:13–14

In John 7, Jesus took the metaphor of water one very big leap
forward:

On the final and climactic day of the Feast, Jesus took his
stand. He cried out, "If anyone thirsts, let him come to me
and drink. Rivers of living water will brim and spill out of
the depths of anyone who believes in me this way, just as the
Scripture says." (He said this in regard to the Spirit, whom
those who believed in him were about to receive).

—JOHN 7:37–39, THE MESSAGE

Jesus was talking about His Spirit—His very life. Paul speaks
about "the spirit of life in Christ Jesus." (See Romans 8:2;
1 Thessalonians 2:13.) You cannot separate the life of God from
the Spirit of God. The Holy Spirit is the living water of God, and
Life[2] is the Spirit-filled life.

Like a battery needing water—acidic water—to fulfill its purpose, you need the Living Water to fulfill your purpose. And that's what the Spirit of God does when He fills us. He activates us to the potential God has placed within us. He energizes us with God's energy, vitality, and wide perspective. The Holy Spirit brings us great gulps of life.

Not long ago, in my devotions, I was thinking about God's name, I Am. It speaks of His eternal aliveness. All that He is, He is right now. He has always been alive, and He is the very fountainhead of life.

Just a sprinkle of that aliveness would ignite Abraham and Sarah's parched, wrinkled bodies and bring about Isaac, the miracle child. That same persistent aliveness would generate the Christ child in the womb of Mary and raise Him from the dead thirty-three years later. That same eternal aliveness has birthed millions of people from every race, tribe, and nation into a never-ending realm of existence and eternal relationship with an eternal God.

When Jesus walked this planet, He told His friend, Martha:

> "I am, right now, Resurrection and Life. The one who believes in me, even though he or she dies, will live. And everyone who lives believing in me does not ultimately die at all."
> —JOHN 11:25–26, THE MESSAGE

Life isn't a philosophy, a belief system, an attitude, a way of thinking, or a set of guiding principles. Life is a Person. Life is Jesus.

Yet at this very moment, men and women, teen guys and teen girls, are scurrying around and scouring the world to find some little shred of life and comfort to cling to. Remember *Cheers*, the old sit-com about life in a local tavern? The lyrics of the program's theme song spoke of going to a place where everyone knows your name and everyone's glad you came.

Excuse me if this sounds too heretical, but wouldn't that be a good theme song for the church of Jesus Christ? Wouldn't it be wonderful if people thought of church as a place where they could bring their heartaches and troubles and worries, where there was plentiful acceptance and true community, and people cared about you, welcomed you, and knew your name?

Even though our Lord's representatives here on earth often get it wrong and fail to welcome wandering souls into "real life," what people all over the world crave and long after and pay such a dreadful price to find is actually closer than they think, where they least expected it, actually in a freely flowing Fountain—so near to hand that if they would listen, they could hear its music.

EVERYONE WANTS MORE LIFE

One of the explorers who shipped out with Christopher Columbus on his second voyage to the New World was a man named Juan Ponce de Leon. This sea-faring man loved the new territories, and asked permission to stay in Hispaniola. On this second journey, he was allowed to do that.

Ponce de Leon became the governor of Puerto Rico in 1508, and while performing the duties of his office in that far frontier, he heard stories about a spring, a mysterious fountain with magic water. According to the strange reports filtering back to him, the water would reverse the effects of aging, and keep a person young forever.

It was called, of course, the Fountain of Youth.

Evidently, it was something the governor could never quite get out of his mind. Finally, leaving his office, his home, and the rudiments of civilization in Puerto Rico, he resolved to find that legendary water source. With the permission of Spanish King Charles, Ponce de Leon set sail in 1513.

He didn't find the fountain, but he did find Florida! He stopped at a pleasant place he named St. Augustine—which became the first Spanish settlement in North America. As he sailed away from his home in Puerto Rico, Ponce de Leon might have been surprised to learn that he would spend the rest of his life looking for the mythical fountain, finally dying in Cuba. And that was the end of his quest.[1]

The end of *his* quest, but not the end of *the* quest. People to this day are searching for the Fountain of Youth. Everyone wants more life. From the perspective of us finite, earth-bound beings, older means less life left, younger means more life left.

One of my colleagues recently said that Abraham and Sarah were wrinkling by the minute. Have you ever felt like that? Just recently in my devotions I read where Scripture refers to Abraham and Sarah as "well-advanced in years" (Gen 18:11). That's not too bad. Abraham could have probably used that expression to describe his wife and it wouldn't have landed him in trouble back at the tent that night. But then I looked at a different translation and it said they were "well stricken in years" (THE MESSAGE). Not so good! That wouldn't be a phrase he would want to toss around too freely in regards to Sarah—or he might find himself stricken!

I recently heard a good-natured put-down of a seventy-something friend. He was introduced like this: "Jack was around when the Dead Sea was only sick!"

For Abraham and Sarah, it certainly must have seemed as though life was going by too fast—along with any opportunity to see God's promise fulfilled in their lives. Have you ever felt that way? Maybe you feel like your life has been depleted or wasted, or is almost over.

You need to understand something. When you tap into life in the Spirit, you tap into timelessness. You tap into eternity.

UNLIMITED LIFE, UNLIMITED IMPACT

$Life^2$ is life that cannot be measured by minutes, hours, and days, because it is the shared resurrection life of God's eternal Son. "He who has the Son has life" (1 John 5:12). This life has a dimension that transcends time itself. What is done, what is said, what is offered, what is accomplished in the power of $Life^2$ cannot be evaluated in mere earthly numbers.

A simple word of counsel can be passed on for generations.

A small deed of kindness, magnified by the math of heaven, might be told in a hundred languages.

A secret gift of money can multiply a thousand-fold.

A Spirit-inspired idea can inflame a whole generation.

When the indwelling life of the Lord Jesus directs, empowers, and animates our daily words and actions, we simply have no concept of the resulting impact.

Think of the woman who broke the alabaster jar of precious perfume, pouring it on the feet of the Lord Jesus, and wiping His feet with her hair. (See Matthew 26:7.) It was a simple, perhaps spontaneous, act of love that probably took no more than five minutes. But echoes of that act have encircled the globe countless times over two millennia. The story of this woman's single act of devotion has been told and retold in almost every known language, in almost every corner of the world, to this day.

The impact of a life has very little to do with the duration of that life. In heaven's view, depth counts more than length or breadth. A few years fully yielded to Christ Jesus and overflowing with Life² can shake the world.

When you tap into the Spirit life, you tap into eternal life. You tap into the timeless dimension. When you tap into a maple tree, you get maple. But when you tap into divine life, you get immortality.

The Bible says that our old lives, when we were living without the indwelling Spirit of God, are like grass:

> The old life is a grass life, its beauty as short-lived as wild-flowers; Grass dries up, flowers droop, God's Word goes on and on forever. This is the Word that conceived the new life in you.
>
> —1 PETER 1:24–2:1, THE MESSAGE

It doesn't matter if you're a big time mover and shaker in this world. It doesn't matter if you've built towering skyscrapers of glass and steel that bear your name or a pyramid the size of a small mountain that covers your remains and molders in the desert for several millennia. It doesn't matter if you've founded a software company, won a beauty contest, or played in the Super Bowl. Life apart from the Fountain of Life is temporary life. James called it "nothing but a wisp of fog, catching a brief bit of sun before disappearing" (4:14, THE MESSAGE).

And that is the very fact Satan uses as a club to beat us down. Our enemy, the serial killer, whispers, "Your life doesn't matter.

You'll never achieve your dreams. There's not enough time left to accomplish anything." What a hellish lie that is.

No matter what your age, no matter how poor your track record, no matter what circumstances in which you find yourself, life changes when you tap into the well of the Living One, who sees you.

LIFE NEVER ENDING

A friend of mine sat by his wife's hospital bed as she was dying of cancer. It seemed to him that her life was just ebbing away—fading, fading, fading, until it was gone. The memories of those moments troubled him deeply. Then one day in his Bible study he came across a passage in 2 Corinthians that changed his whole perspective on that agonizing time.

Speaking of physical death, Paul wrote, "For while we are in this tent [our physical body], we groan, and are burdened, because we do not wish to be unclothed but to be clothed with our heavenly dwelling [our new body], so that what is mortal may be swallowed up by life" (2 Cor. 5:4).

"Swallowed up by life." Suddenly it hit this grieving man that it hadn't been death pressing into that room, but *Life!* Life kept pressing in and pressing in until it finally swallowed her up into never-ending life, healing, and sheer gladness of heart.

There's something better—infinitely better than the Fountain of Youth. It is the *Fountain of Life.* If Ponce de Leon had actually found his mythical well, drank from its waters, and lived to this day, he would be the most miserable man on the planet. What a terror and horror it would be to have centuries and millennia of human life on this sick, broken world of ours. Think of all the wars, betrayals, injustices, and sorrows his eyes would have beheld. That's why, after Adam and Eve sinned, God blocked the way to the Tree of Life. It wouldn't have been mercy at all to let them live forever on a world under a curse.

Life^2 is infinitely better. While we live on this world, we have purpose, meaning, and day-by-day contact and friendship with the "Prince of Life" (Acts 3:15, NKJV). Then in just a little while, our mortal life is swallowed up by life eternal—not on an unhappy planet under the shadow of death, but in the kingdom of light, where no shadow will ever dim the eternal morning, and no thief will ever steal your joy.

CHAPTER 7

DEAD MEN WALKING

God reveals Himself to us one obedience at a time.

Most of us can recall times in our walk with Christ when we've been leaning against some usually closed-and-locked door in our understanding and it suddenly swings wide open. Where there were once unyielding locks and deadbolts, now a simple push gives full access. Something has opened up in our mind, in our spirit, and we almost lurch into that new room of truth.

It is the Holy Spirit who opens such doors, and He opens them most often to those who continually ask, seek, and knock. Those who most deeply want to live by revelation will find that desire fulfilled.

If you're anything like me, you'd like to linger for awhile in the warmth and radiance of those revelations and divine disclosures. Maybe pitch a tent on that high and holy ground for a time and bask in the glory, as Peter proposed on the Mount of Transfiguration. (See Mark 9:5.)

But that's not the way God usually works.

He doesn't let us stay on the mountaintop.

He doesn't let us revel in knowledge for knowledge's sake.

At some point, we have to walk down the mountainside to confront what's happening in the valley of everyday life. At that point, we learn whether that new understanding of ours will be filed away on the bookshelf of promising-but-barely-relevant information, or whether we will put it to work for the kingdom of light in a dark world.

In other words, after the lecture, you have a lab. After the class time, you have an exam, and sometimes when you least expect it.

Abraham had received his "A-H degree," but there were more tests to come. In fact, the biggest test of his life.

FINAL EXAM

> Some time later God tested Abraham. He said to him, "Abraham!" "Here I am," he replied. Then God said, "Take your son, your only son, Isaac, whom you love, and go to the region of Moriah. Sacrifice him there as a burnt offering on one of the mountains I will tell you about."
>
> —GENESIS 22:1–2

Isaac was the very essence and embodiment of Life² to Abraham—his long-delayed dream, his miracle son, his blessing, his future, his legacy, his life.

Isaac was *laughter*. That was the young man's name, and that's what he meant to Abraham and Sarah. Hilarity. Bubbling joy. Sheer delight. A song in the heart. Purpose for living. At this point in the Genesis account, "Laughter" would have been twenty-seven years old. A full-grown man. His father and mother would have watched him grow through boyhood into a sturdy young man in his prime. No doubt they had begun to wonder about a bride for their son and grandchildren to follow.

But now, it seemed, that wasn't to be. Abraham, who had walked with God under the stars, now watched those stars wink out, one by one. God was asking him to lay down everything pertaining to hope and happiness in his life.

Most of us have an Isaac or two in our lives. Not a literal son or daughter, perhaps, but one thing that best represents our future, our hopes, our dreams, and our joy in life. Though we may never say it out loud, our heart says, "I live for this."

Now imagine God asking you to hand that over to Him. It's that last thing you'd expect. It's unimaginable.

"WHERE IS THE LAMB?"

The Lord had said to Abraham, "Sacrifice him there as a burnt offering." Now there is a word we don't like. Sacrifice. We shun it, shrink from it, shove it away. But the Bible says that after Abraham received this crushing word from the Lord, he didn't waste any time, mount any defense, or find excuses to delay:

> Early the next morning Abraham got up and saddled his donkey. He took with him two of his servants and his son Isaac. When he had cut enough wood for the burnt offering, he set out for the place God had told him about. On the third day Abraham looked up and saw the place in the distance. He said to his servants, "Stay here with the donkey while I and the boy go over there. We will worship and then we will come back to you."
>
> —GENESIS 22: 3–5

Abraham and his son hiked up that rocky peak together—
Mount Moriah, which means, "God sees and approves."

Isaac, of course, had been through this drill many times before.
He knew about sacrifices. He knew that he was carrying the wood
for the burnt offering on his back, and that his dad was bearing
a torch and a knife for killing the sacrificial animal. The fact that
they had come so far and that his father seemed so grave on the
journey must have tipped the young man off that this sacrifice
was something beyond the ordinary.

Even so, something was missing.

> Isaac spoke up and said to his father Abraham, "Father?" "Yes,
> my son?" Abraham replied. "The fire and wood are here,"
> Isaac said, "but where is the lamb for the burnt offering?"
> Abraham answered, "God himself will provide the lamb for
> the burnt offering, my son." And the two of them went on
> together. When they reached the place God had told him
> about, Abraham built an altar there and arranged the wood
> on it. He bound his son Isaac and laid him on the altar, on
> top of the wood. Then he reached out his hand and took the
> knife to slay his son.
>
> —GENESIS 22:7–10

There is a universe of revelation between the words, "God will
provide the lamb" and "he bound his son Isaac and laid him on
the altar." I think that's what Bible meditation is all about. You
and I study and ponder the actual words and lines of Scripture,
but we also think about what's *between* those lines. And we need
to place ourselves in the stories.

Scripture gives us a simple, bare-bones account, but we can
only imagine the emotion and the agony that throbs within this
narrative. Abraham was prepared to sacrifice his beloved son,

and it would have been a far, far easier task for the old man to plunge the knife into his own chest. For his part, Abraham's son submitted to being bound, and to lying down on top of the wood on the altar. No doubt he could have easily refused, easily overpowered his father—"Are you kidding? Have you lost your mind, Dad? This is crazy!"—and simply walked away.

But Isaac trusted his father and his father's God. In later years, God allowed Himself to be called "the Fear of Isaac" (Gen. 31:42). Perhaps at that moment, when Isaac willingly crawled up onto the rough stone altar and offered his young life, God became the God of Isaac as well as the God of Abraham.

WHEN GOD STEPS IN

Sometimes I've wished I could have a CD of their conversation up on that bleak mountaintop. Or were there any words spoken at all? Truthfully, it was more than a conversation, it was a lifestyle. Isaac knew that his dad had not only talked his faith through the years, he had *walked* his faith. If Abraham said he had heard a word from God—even when it seemed wildly illogical—then Isaac was ready to follow.

That's something to think about in our parenting. It isn't showing up at church every time the door opens that impresses our children, it is our faith—exercised in both the thoroughfares and back alleys, in the highs and lows of life. As the old saying goes, "What you do speaks louder than what you say."

Never doubt that your kids are watching your life—watching to see if there is a consistency between what you say you believe and how you actually live it out day by day. In fact, our children are much more likely to become what we *are* than what we say.

When Abraham and his son arrived together at that mountaintop, Isaac was ready to say words like these, even through his tears: "I believe like you do, Dad. I believe that God is so bountiful, so alive, that if I give my own life, He'll give me back more than I give."

Verse 10 says Abraham "reached out his hand and took the knife to slay his son." Can you picture it? The knife raised in the air, the morning sunlight glinting from the naked blade. But then God stepped in.

> But the angel of the Lord called out to him from heaven, "Abraham! Abraham!" "Here I am," he replied. "Do not lay a hand on the boy," he said. "Do not do anything to him. Now I know that you fear God, because you have not withheld from me your son, your only son."
>
> —GENESIS 22:11–12

"Your only son." It's like John 3:16—a preview of the cross. "For God so loved the world that he gave his one and only Son, that whoever believes in him shall not perish but have eternal life."

> Abraham looked up and there in a thicket he saw a ram caught by its horns. He went over and took the ram and sacrificed it as a burnt offering instead of his son. So Abraham called that place The Lord Will Provide. And to this day it is said, "On the mountain of the Lord it will be provided."
>
> —GENESIS 22:13–14

If God already knew what was going to happen on that mountain, did Abraham's act of faith still move Him? You can bank on it. It moved Him. It touched God's great heart in an especially tender place. He is moved by our faith. He is *pleased* by our faith. "And without faith it is impossible to please God" (Heb. 11:6).

God was saying to Abraham, "Now I know that you understand who I am, because you are willing to let go of your Isaac. In that, Abraham, you're a lot like Me." Many Bible scholars believe that Mount Moriah is the same mountain on which Jerusalem sits, and where Christ laid down His life on Golgotha.

"God himself will provide the lamb for the burnt offering, my son."

And John the Baptist said of Jesus: "Behold, the Lamb of God!" (John 1:36, KJV). Jesus is the Lamb that God Himself provided for Abraham, Isaac, and the whole world. When Abraham looked up and saw the ram caught in the thicket, he took his knife and sacrificed the ram instead of his son.

A NEW NAME FOR GOD

Through an excruciating experience of faith and obedience in the laboratory of life, Abraham was about to learn something about his God. He named the place where the angel of the Lord had stayed his hand, "The Lord Will Provide." It's actually a name of God, *Yahweh Jirah*, or *Jehovah Jirah*. God is a providing God, and He revealed Himself to Abraham in a new way.

Here's what I have found in my walk with God over the past thirty-seven years: the more you find out about God, the more you find out about *you*. The more you see and understand who He is and what He is like, the more you see and understand who you really are—what He had in mind when He created you and put you on this planet. Find out the names of God, and you'll find out *your* real name.

The fact is, God reveals Himself to us one obedience at a time. You hear Him speak to you, one obedience at a time. Revelation is incremental—contingent on obeying the last thing He said to me. If Abraham hadn't followed through on God's command to sacrifice Isaac, he would probably have never understood God to be Yahweh Jirah, the God who provides.

Perhaps you have never found out how God provides in your life, because you've never let go of your Isaac. You've never experienced life at a higher level because you've never trusted God enough to let go of life on *this* level. He can't put new things into your hands, because your fingers are clenched around all that you have right now.

Speaking of the Father's provision, the Lord Jesus said:

> "Don't worry about having enough food or drink or clothing. Why be like the pagans who are so deeply concerned about these things? Your heavenly Father already knows all your needs, and he will give you all you need from day to day if you live for him and make the Kingdom of God your primary concern."
> —MATTHEW 6:31–33, AUTHOR'S PARAPHRASE

Even so, it's hard for us to let go. And no one said letting go would be easy. No one said receiving the overflow of God's life within you would be a downhill stroll. No matter what some name-it-and-claim-it preachers might tell you, Life² isn't some complimentary plane ticket to the Bahamas. There are some gut-wrenching, Mount Moriah experiences along the way.

Jesus said, "If you cling to your life, you will lose it; but if you give it up for me, you will save it" (Matt. 10:39, TLB). Why do we cling? Why do we keep a white knuckle grip on everything that seems so worthwhile and precious to us? Why do we guard it even from the Lord? Because we're really not ready to trust Him.

We're not ready to believe that life is found in surrender because our natural tendency and the prevailing world philosophy says, "Don't let go." We don't expect birth to take place in a graveyard, and we don't expect to find life by letting go of the title to our dreams and ourselves.

The New Testament tells us that Abraham was ready to offer Isaac, figuring that, "If God wanted to, he could raise the dead. In a sense, that's what happened when he received Isaac back, alive from off the altar" (Heb. 11:17, THE MESSAGE). This grieving dad had no real clue what God was going to do or how He was going to do it. He knew that his descendents would (somehow) come through Isaac, but he couldn't really imagine how that would happen. He had no way of foreseeing that an angel of the Lord would suddenly stop him with a shout from heaven.

He couldn't connect the dots at that point. He didn't know how it would work, and he didn't *have to* know how it would work. He just knew that God was big enough to do it—to do *anything*—and that the Faithful One would never be less than faithful to His promise.

And so he stepped right off the cliff.

Life² isn't just a bonus laid on top of your present life. It's an *exchange*. Your life for His. Your priorities for His. Your dreams for His. Your plans for His. Your way of figuring out life for His. And you're not going to make the exchange while you're holding on to what you already have. You have to lay it down.

Like Abraham.

Like Isaac.

Like Jesus.

THE ANGEL'S SECOND WORD

The angel of the Lord called to Abraham from heaven a second time and said, "I swear by myself, declares the Lord, that because you have done this and have not withheld your son, your only son, I will surely bless you and make your descendants as numerous as the stars in the sky and as the sand on the seashore. Your descendants will take possession of the cities of their enemies, and through your offspring all nations on earth will be blessed, because you have obeyed me."

—GENESIS 22:15–18

Is it significant that the angel of the Lord called out to Abraham a second time? I think it might be. The first time, He stayed Abraham's hand, and said, "Do not lay a hand on the boy.... Do not do anything to him."

Then the old patriarch looked up and saw God's provision, God's chosen sacrifice ready to be offered in Isaac's stead. As the smoke from the altar ascended to heaven, Abraham saw God through new eyes—most likely streaming with tears of gratitude. He understood God's heart and His purposes in a deeper, more profound way than he had ever grasped them before.

He had met God-my-Provider—Yahweh Jirah—on that mountaintop. And as that wondrous knowledge settled into his consciousness, God began to release a mighty river of blessing.

If you are a believer today, it is because God called you and wooed you through His Holy Spirit, and you responded. But that's as far as many believers will go in this life. They will never experience the confidence, the exhilaration, and the wider, higher vistas of Life^2.

If Abraham had decided not to obey, he wouldn't have experienced those things either. But when he followed God into the darkness, when he laid his greatest treasure on the altar, he experienced God at a new level, and came to know Him by another name.

And when the angel called out to him a second time, it was with the promise of blessing greater than the man could have dreamed or imagined.

Abraham would be prosperous. Successful. Victorious in battle. And through His offspring, all the nations on earth through all generations until the end of time would taste the overflow of that blessings. If that isn't Life², then I don't know what is.

Where then, do you and I fit into this story? We *do* fit, you know. This story wasn't placed in Scripture to entertain us or to make us say, "Wow, what a great guy Abraham was." No, the story is there to teach us, to help us to move into a deeper walk with our God, and to lead us from life to Life².

The Bible tells us, "Now these things happened to them as an example, and they were written for our instruction, upon whom the ends of the ages have come" (1 Cor. 10:11, NAS).

God knew we would need this story, and He wants us to put ourselves in Abraham's place and ask ourselves, "Could I do what Abraham did? Can I obey like that? Can I lay my most precious possessions on the altar of faith?"

Why is the Bible composed of story after story, rather than some long recitation of rules? Because we understand life by means of stories, and when we put ourselves into the story, we experience its maximum benefit.

"MORE AND BETTER"

Why are so few of Jesus' followers actually experiencing the fullness of the "more and better" life He promised in John 10:10? It may be because we're not willing to pay the price. And we don't want anything to do with sacrifice.

The same Jesus who uttered that verse in the gospel of John, also voiced the words in Matthew 10:39: "Whoever finds his life will lose it, and whoever loses his life for my sake will find it." You don't get His life until you let go of your life. You don't find Him as your Yahweh-Jirah until you let go of your Isaacs. And just as God tested His servant Abraham, so He tests all of His servants. Our very lives are a test. And like Abraham, we can pass the test and walk into His over-the-top blessing and provision for our lives.

Here's how.

1. Follow the Leader

To let go of Isaac, Abraham had to be convinced that more life is available to those who sacrifice, surrender, and serve, than to those who are selfish and cling to their precious possessions. Abraham passed the test, and we can follow in his footsteps.

In fact, God passed His own test. He gave His only Son, His Isaac, His greatest joy, His very life. The cross wasn't a mistake or a miscalculation. Isaiah 53:10 tells us that it was the very thing God had in mind all along. The plan was that He would give Himself as an offering for sin, knowing that as a result, life would burst forth like a vast torrent of light and joy, thundering over the floodgates of heaven.

The plan was that He give Himself as an offering for sin so that He'd see life come from it—life, life, and more life. And God's plan will deeply prosper through Him.

> Let us fix our eyes on Jesus, the author and perfecter of our faith, who for the joy set before him endured the cross, scorning its shame, and sat down at the right hand of the throne of God.
>
> —HEBREWS 12:2

Why did Jesus endure the cross? Why did He embrace the sacrifice? For the *joy* that awaited Him. What joy? The joy of resurrection. The joy of having a relationship with you! He thought of you when He went to the cross. And with you in mind—your rescue, your salvation, your eternal destiny—He passed the test. And so can you.

2. Practice letting go

When you tap into unlimited generosity, it makes you generous. If you're a stingy person, you don't know Yahweh Jirah yet. When you find out who God is, how generous He is, and what an abundant full-of-life God He is, then you will give life away. You won't have a scarcity mentality.

Believe! Let go! It's one thing to let go of your Ishmael, your mistake, your problem, but it's a whole other ball game when God starts asking for your Isaac—the very thing He gave you and blessed you with. So Abraham prepared to sacrifice his son, and he was about to drive one final stake through the heart of selfishness.

I was reading in my devotions the other day about God's plan for a "year of jubilee" in the national life of Israel. (See Leviticus 25.) Every fifty years, all debts were to be cancelled, and all properties returned to the ancestral owners. It didn't matter what your current balance sheet might read in year forty-nine, in year fifty everything was zeroed out. On New Year's day of the fiftieth year, you'd wake up in the morning owing nothing to anyone, and with no one owing anything to you. All debts disappeared with the turn of that calendar page.

I couldn't help wondering what that would look like in the United States. The closest thing we have to it today is bankruptcy, but that's a negative example. In the Year of Jubilee, no one was a debtor and no one was a creditor. Everyone went back to equal footing with each other and before the Lord, or—at least that's how God intended it to work.

Think of a Monopoly game. At the end of the contest, you have millionaires and paupers, tycoons and beggars, Donald Trumps and Forrest Gumps. But then the game is over and it all goes back into the box.

That's how it will be for all of us one day. Time will be up for us, and all our earthly assets will go back into the box. We won't be able to carry one penny into eternity. We'll leave behind all our property, all our earthly investments, all our bank accounts, and every last one of our possessions.

In view of these things, the best and wisest thing we can possibly do is *practice* giving it away right now—investing our assets in those accounts beyond earth that will never lose their value.

I recently performed a funeral for a member of our church. He had just become a vice president of a company with over twenty thousand employees. But he died relatively young, and everything he'd accumulated went back into the box.

Practice letting go. Jesus let go of His life, and He got resurrection—and you in the bargain. And as you let go of your own life, you'll find life times life—Life².

> "If your first concern is to look after yourself, you'll never find yourself. But if you forget about yourself and look to me, you'll find both yourself and me."
> —MATTHEW 10:39, THE MESSAGE

As I write these words, I'm looking at a tiny sunflower seed in the palm of my hand. If I plant this seed in the fertile Oregon soil, I can get a sunflower and many, many more seeds. But if I don't plant it, if I don't sacrifice it and commit it to the soil, I'll be left with one lonely seed, and that's all.

Every seed has a promise. Every sunflower seed has a promise of towering flowers, turning their faces to the sun and fairly bursting with seeds. Every Isaac has a promise of life in it, but you've got to plant it! You've got to bury the Isaac; you've got to let go. Jesus said:

> "Listen carefully: Unless a grain of wheat is buried in the ground, dead to the world, it is never any more than a grain of wheat. But if it is buried, it sprouts and reproduces itself many times over. In the same way, anyone who holds on to life just as it is destroys that life. But if you let it go, reckless in your love, you'll have it forever, real and eternal."
> —JOHN 12:24, THE MESSAGE

What seed was Jesus referring to? Isaac? Yes. Himself? Yes. Me? Yes. You? Yes. You have a promise of life in you: but that promise is not going to become a reality unless you're willing to let go of your own life, and be buried.

"Anyone who holds on to life just as it is destroys that life. But if you let it go, reckless in your love, you'll have it forever, real and eternal."

How do we do that? What does that look like? Listen to the apostle Paul:

> So here's what I want you to do, God helping you: Take your everyday, ordinary life—your sleeping, eating, going-to-work, and walking-around life—and place it before God as an offering.
>
> —ROMANS 12:1, THE MESSAGE

"Take your ordinary, everyday life, waking or sleeping, and place that before your God as an offering." The King James Version says, "Present your bodies a living sacrifice."

There's that word again. Sacrifice. Life^2 is living a sacrificial life; moment by moment laying every thought, every decision, every action, and every impulse on the altar. And the more you offer to Him, the more life you give away, the more you get.

DEAD MEN WALKING?

True Christ-followers are dead men walking, dead women walking. Yet no one could be more alive! As Paul expressed it, "It is no longer I who live, but Christ lives in me. So I live in this earthly body by trusting in the Son of God, who loved me and gave himself for me" (Gal. 2:20, NLT). Jesus Himself was a dead man walking on the afternoon of that first Easter. He wasn't a ghost. Far from it. In fact, resurrection life radiated from His every pore. In the book of Revelation he declares, "I am the living one. I died, but look—I am alive forever and ever! And I hold the keys of death and the grave" (Rev. 1:18, NLT).

Have you ever found yourself staring physical death in the eyes? A few years ago I was chukar hunting on the steep slopes of the Snake River, in a remote, incredibly rugged area called Hell's Canyon. Nobody else in my party wanted to go on that particular slope. For good reason! It was very steep. But the chukars were there—I could hear them! And when I get into the hunting mode, I sometimes become just a little intense. Both my dogs went with me with no hesitation, but my friends went another direction. As I was traversing the steep slope, however, my feet slipped out from under me, and I started to slide. I thought to myself, "It's okay, I'll stop in a few seconds." But I didn't. In fact, I picked up more and more speed, heading for a sheer 80-foot cliff with jagged rocks below.

I could see myself going right over that cliff. What was there to stop me? As I swept along toward that edge, I had the presence of mind to pray, "Oh God, if I'm going over this thing, please let me die, and not be wounded." And then at the last moment I cried aloud: "Jesus!"

On the very edge of that precipice, I hit a rock the size and shape of an orange traffic cone. Actually, I straddled it—right in my crotch—with my legs dangling in empty space. Not the most desirable way to stop a fall, perhaps, but it saved my life. In God's mercy, I was able to inch my way backwards, find some footing, and ever-so-carefully clamber my way back up the incline to safety.

It's interesting what you find yourself thinking when you come that close to death and eternity. We get a taste of it, perhaps, at a funeral. Beyond the sadness of a friend or relative departing this world, we gain an altered perspective of reality—a wake-up call—regarding the fragility of this life and the nearness of the next.

Abraham and Isaac had such a near-death experience as they topped the mountain called Moriah, "God sees and approves." In mere moments, they would experience Easter power a couple of millennia before Easter.

But there is no Easter, there is no resurrection, apart from death. And the Christian life is all about picking up our cross and following Jesus, dying a thousand little deaths to our flesh, to our own desires, every day. Choosing not to be selfish, not to please ourselves, but to sacrifice, surrender, serve, and lay down our lives for others. Do the little tasks that no one sees. It's a moment-by-moment decision.

This may sound strange to you, but I am literally at my best when I'm as good as dead. God wants to free us from addiction to self, and to fully experience Life^2, I must become a living sacrifice. In Gods' plan, the "deader" you are, the better you are! The deader you are, the more alive you are. Dead to self; alive to Him.

You won't be taught that at Harvard or Yale. A professor who stood up at a state school and taught this stuff would be laughed (or forced) off campus. The world says one thing about where to find life. The Word of God says the opposite—that real life is found in the last place you'd expect it.

According to Jesus Christ, dead men walking don't miss out! He said:

> "I tell you the truth . . . no one who has left home or brothers or sisters or mother or father or children or fields for me and the gospel will fail to receive a hundred times as much in this present age (homes, brothers, sisters, mothers,

children and fields—and with them, persecutions) and in the age to come, eternal life."

—MARK 10:29–30, NLT

We need to learn the true "new math"—*kingdom* math. Whatever we lay on the altar now for Jesus' sake, will come back multiplied beyond all calculation. We will walk in Life[2] here on earth, and experience even more life—endless, exponential life—after this life.

Abraham offered his best, and Yahweh-Jirah not only returned what he'd offered, but upped the ante a trillion times over.

After all, God invented giving, and no one does it better.

CHAPTER 8

A BETTER COUNTRY

The ultimate definition of Life^2 is simply being with Jesus.

When Jesus said, "I came so they can have real and eternal life, more and better life than they ever dreamed of" (John 10:10, THE MESSAGE), was He speaking of something here and now, or something out beyond us, in eternity?

The answer is *yes*.

The answer is *both*.

Something incomparable happens the moment you receive the living Lord Jesus Christ into your life. From then on, the life of God Himself—the One who cannot die—flows in and through your life, a fast running river, bringing you the capacity to live at a higher level than you "ever dreamed of."

That's Life^2.

It's a life that begins on earth and continues forever.

Does that mean life here on earth will always be like a stroll through the rose garden? No, not at all. The fact is, it hasn't always been an easy passage for God's children on this world so marred and dominated by the evil one. Jesus Himself promised persecutions, trouble, and sorrow. In Hebrews 11, the writer describes those who were harassed and hounded for their allegiance to Christ.

> There were those who, under torture, refused to give in and go free, preferring something better: resurrection. Others braved abuse and whips, and, yes, chains and dungeons. We have stories of those who were stoned, sawed in two, murdered in cold blood; stories of vagrants wandering the earth in animal skins, homeless, friendless, powerless—the world didn't deserve them!—making their way as best they could on the cruel edges of the world.
> —HEBREWS 11:35–38, THE MESSAGE

What about Life^2 for these men and women? Did their files get lost somewhere in some celestial bureaucracy? Did God overlook them? Did they somehow slip through the system and get shortchanged? Where was *their* "more and better" life?

It was there.

It never left them for a moment.

Wherever these Christ-followers walked, the Son of God walked with them, step for step. He was at their side in the dungeons, in the caves, and on the run through wild and rugged wilderness. And they wouldn't have traded the nearness of Jesus Christ for all the comfort, luxury, and soft living in the world! With Moses, they "regarded disgrace for the sake of Christ as of greater value than the treasures of Egypt" (Heb. 11:26). And bear in mind that the treasures of Egypt were vast beyond measure and comprehension.

And that's not all.

They not only knew Jesus up-close-and-personal, they saw something in the distance. Something shimmering on a far horizon. And it drew their hearts like metal filings to a strong magnet. The writer says that "they were longing for a better country—a heavenly one" (Heb. 11:16).

It's always "a good country" when you experience that indescribable presence of the living God, and find yourself filled to overflowing with His Holy Spirit.

But there are even better times coming.

A better country awaits our arrival.

Someday heaven! I love that thought. That's part of my inheritance.

> This resurrection life you received from God is not a timid, grave-tending life. It's adventurously expectant, greeting God with a childlike "What's next, Papa?" God's Spirit touches our spirits and confirms who we really are. We know who he is, and we know who we are: Father and children. And we know we are going to get what's coming to us—an unbelievable inheritance!
> —ROMANS 8:15–17, THE MESSAGE

Jesus said, "There are many homes up there where my Father lives, and I am going to prepare them for your coming. When everything is ready, then I will come and get you, so that you can always be with me where I am" (John 14:2–3, TLB).

That last part is most significant.

"So that you can always be with me where I am."

That's the best definition of Life[2] that there ever was. "Being with Jesus." He is Life. He is Truth. He is Peace. He is Love. He is Joy. He is Beauty. He is Light. He is Wonder. He is Kindness. He is Strength. He is Wisdom. He is everything that has ever made life worth living. Heaven is wherever He is. Hell is wherever He is not.

Life² here on earth simply means walking in the life and savoring the intimacy with the Son of God. The more you do that, the higher your life goes. The more you neglect to seek Him and receive His life-flow, the more your life will seem empty, trivial, and boring.

And Life² beyond our lifespan here on earth? It's Life to the zillionth power. Because we will see Him, feel His touch, hear His voice, watch the expressions play across His face, walk at His side on excursions through endless galaxies.

It's as simple as this.

Life² is Jesus.

NOTES

Chapter 1
A Modest Proposal

1. Bible verse in Bulgarian available at http://www.biblegateway.com/versions/index.php?action=getVersionInfo&vid=21&lang=26 (accessed Nov. 15, 2007).

Chapter 2
A Walk Under the Stars

1. F. LaGard Smith, *The Narrated Bible in Chronological Order* (Eugene, OR: Harvest House Publishers, 1984).

2. *Modern Language Bible* (Grand Rapids, MI: Zondervan Publishers, 1969), 10.

3. Ron Mehl, *God Works the Night Shift* (Multnomah, OR: Multnomah Publishers, 1995).

Chapter 4
Death Grip

1. William Ernest Henley, from the poem "Inviticus," http://www.poetryloverspage.com/poets/henley/henley_ind.html (accessed November 5, 2007).

2. C.S. Lewis, *The Lion, the Witch, and the Wardrobe,* the first volume from the set *The Chronicles of Narnia* (New York, NY: HarperCollins Publishers, 1977), 75–76.

Chapter 6
Fountain of Youth

1. "Ponce de Leon and the Search for the Fountain of Youth," http://en.wikipedia.org/wiki/Juan_Ponce_de_Le%C3%B3n (accessed November 5, 2007).